Love Yourself

Ways to Loving Yourself Like Your Life Depends on It

(Become a Self Worth and Confident Woman Affirmations and Quotes)

Jason Hills

Published By **John Kembrey**

Jason Hills

All Rights Reserved

Love Yourself: Ways to Loving Yourself Like Your Life Depends on It (Become a Self Worth and Confident Woman Affirmations and Quotes)

ISBN 978-1-77485-866-0

No part of this guidebook shall be reproduced in any form without permission in writing from the publisher except in the case of brief quotations embodied in critical articles or reviews.

Legal & Disclaimer

The information contained in this ebook is not designed to replace or take the place of any form of medicine or professional medical advice. The information in this ebook has been provided for educational & entertainment purposes only.

The information contained in this book has been compiled from sources deemed reliable, and it is accurate to the best of the Author's knowledge; however, the Author cannot guarantee its accuracy and validity and cannot be held liable for any errors or omissions. Changes are periodically made to this book. You must consult your doctor or get professional medical advice before using any of the suggested remedies, techniques, or information in this book.

Upon using the information contained in this book, you agree to hold harmless the Author from and against any damages, costs, and expenses, including any legal fees potentially resulting from the application of any of the information provided by this guide. This disclaimer applies to any damages or injury caused by the use and application, whether directly or indirectly, of any advice or information presented, whether for breach of contract, tort, negligence, personal injury, criminal intent, or under any other cause of action.

You agree to accept all risks of using the information presented inside this book. You need to consult a professional medical practitioner in order to ensure you are both able and healthy enough to participate in this program.

TABLE OF CONTENTS

Introduction 1

Chapter 1: What Is The Reason Some People Love Their Self More Than Others? 2

Chapter 2: What Is It Really Mean To Love Yourself? 7

Chapter 3: To Create Inner Peace Using Mindfulness Meditation? 11

Chapter 4: Everyone Is Hurt 37

Chapter 5: The Mountain Of Wisdom 78

Chapter 6: Unstoppable Confidence 103

Chapter 7: What Is It Mean To Love Yourself 150

Conclusion 183

Introduction

The book offers practical steps and strategies on how to get rid of your fears and negative self-image and live a more meaningful life.

It is claimed that you cannot be loved by anyone else until you love yourself. The phrase is frequently used in TV shows and often found in books, and it is now a common occurrence however what is it that really means to be self-love? The book below will assist you to comprehend how self-love is defined, and will provide answers to the most frequently asked questions about self-love. There are also techniques can be applied to improve confidence in yourself, self confidence, and self-love.

This book will allow you to recognize yourself more and be your own best friend. It will help you increase your self-esteem and self-worth to help you create healthier and more satisfying relationships and lead a life that is filled with joy and confidence.

I hope you enjoy it!

Chapter 1: What Is The Reason Some People Love Their Self More Than Others?

Self-love is a rabid trending word in the present. It is widely discussed in a variety of psychology books, and is the talk of talk shows such as Oprah. Numerous psychologists believe that self-love is the key to happiness and achievement in life. Self-love, however, isn't something we are born with. Self-love is influenced by our environment, social contexts as well as our perceptions of others and our childhood. This is the reason certain individuals love themselves more than other people.

The concept of self-love was invented by a renowned psychologist, named Erich Fromm. Erich Fromm proposed that loving self-love is distinct from narcissism and conceit. The degree of love one has to himself is greatly affected by his self-worth as well as self-confidence, self-respect, and self-esteem. Individuals who believe that they are worthy as well-deserving of affection will tend to appreciate themselves more. Self-esteem sufferersworth, on the contrary tend to be self-deprecating because they don't believe they deserve the love and affection of others, or even from them. People who are confident in their capabilities and feel confident about their self-worth are happier than people who lack self-esteem.

Apart from having a good self-esteem and self worth, many people who feel they are loved were raised in a warm and supportive home where self-love is encouraged. The people who have a healthy self-love as they grow older typically have extremely caring and supportive parents. They were raised in a loving and nurturing family where they were valued and respected as they are. Self-loved people are raised in a family where it's okay to make mistakes, and they are loved for who they are. People who are more self-love are raised in a place that is safe and secure.

One reason why certain individuals love themselves more than others is the different mental conditioning. Some people are taught from their families or other authority individuals to believe they aren't worthy of being loved. Here are a few reasons why people may have trouble loving themselves

1. They were often criticized for their actions when they were children. Those who are self-defying and aren't able to love themselves are often criticized by parents or other authority individuals. They often face punishment whenever you make the tiniest error. They also are often assaulted physically and emotionally. If a person is frequently neglected and mistreated by those that are expected to give them that love they deserve, they will believe that they don't merit being loved. They are likely to have low self-esteem, and may struggle to show the love and respect to themselves.

2. They were abused as children - people who struggle to love themselves are usually raised by parents who are constantly neglecting their requirements. Children who were abandoned by their parents at a young age, spend the rest of their life thinking about the reason they were left to their parent's care. It's difficult to feel loved by

them because they don't understand what it means to be loved from the beginning.

3. They were raised in a solitary home. Some have the privilege of having loving parents, but there are children who suffer from parents who constantly fight one another. If someone was raised in a household where there was a lot of conflicts, it can be difficult to be loved by them.

4. They have experienced traumatic experiences when they were victimized as a child, or is the victim of a crime that is heinous it will be difficult for him to accept the world around him and his. Victims of abuse usually blame themselves.

5. The idea of loving oneself is disallowed by their religion . Even at the age of 21 there are still religious groups which have a traditional belief system. They teach that it's not a good idea to love oneself. They were taught that it's selfish to love yourself. This is why certain people develop a sense of codependency by putting others' demands over their own.

6. Media portray certain traits as "lovable"

The media can have a profound influence on people's self confidence and self-worth. Through these media outlets, individuals are convinced that if they don't behave in a certain way or behave in a certain manner that they are not worth the love and respect of others.

The opinions and voices of those that we cherish and admire are important to us. When you're a kid and are constantly criticized by those people who matter to you, it can frequently increase the intensity of your critic and regularly criticize yourself well. The ability of us to be self-love and respect is greatly influenced by self-esteem and self-worth. Individuals who feel insecure about themselves may find self-love quite difficult. But, those who have been raised in a safe and loving family environment are able to respect, love and be kind to themselves. Self-love is an inherent part of them.

Chapter 2: What Is It Really Mean To Love Yourself?

Self-love was first presented by a well-known German psychologist known as Erich Fromm in his 1956 book, The Art of Loving. According To Fromm self-love is distinct from arrogance, narcissism, self-centeredness or pride. In general, there are four main elements or components of love: respect responsibility, concern, and understanding. Love for oneself involves respecting oneself, taking care about yourself, being intimately aware accepting oneself, and being accountable for self-care. Fromm first made popular the saying "In order to truly love someone else, you need to first love yourself".

Self-love can be easy for some individuals, and quite challenging for others because of their environment and their cultural influences. What does self-love actually appear like?

When you're in love with yourself, you're gentle with yourself. You don't beat yourself up too much when you do make an error. When you're in love with yourself, it is easy to forgive yourself for any horrible thing you may have committed over the years. If you are in love with yourself, you are able to avoid working overly hard until you are exhausted. You are mindful of your body's limitations and limits. If you're in love with yourself you eat nutritious foods since you realize that your body requires proper nutrition in order to function optimally.

If you are in love with yourself, you don't ignore it. Do you take supplements regularly to boost your immunity? Do you drink medicine whenever you're required? Do you often visit the salon to get a manicure or cut? Do you regularly work out to ensure that you're fit and healthy? Love yourself by taking proper care of your appearance as well as your body. It is about making sure you appear your best all often. This means you pay attention to your physical, emotional and spiritual requirements.

If you are in love with yourself, you love yourself fully. If you are in love with yourself, you love yourself quite a bit.

You're comfortable with the person you are. You love your appearance and your manner of conduct. If you are happy with yourself, you will not speak harshly towards yourself. You don't make yourself feel bad or label yourself "fat" or "ugly". Psychologists have stated that our body and mind are in some way connected. So if you are positive and are positive regarding your physique, you will prosper.

If you are in love with yourself, you will not make yourself feel bad about yourself like "You are dumb" or "You can never accomplish things right". When you're in love with yourself you establish a routine to be affirmative and constantly use positive words for yourself. Being self-love means that you do not criticize or diminish your capabilities. You believe in yourself and your ability. You are proud of yourself and take care of yourself like your most trusted friend.

Being yourself is also a sign that you've got healthy boundaries. You are not a victim of other people and don't allow others to profit from you. You will not accept any kind of abuse or ill treatment from other people. You define what you can do to help others and what you shouldn't do. You'll begin to establish relationships based on trust, respect and friendship.

If you're in love with yourself you care for your health and your life generally. You make sure your home is cozy and tidy. You maintain a good standard of hygiene. You are comfortable, clean and decent clothing. You strive to be the best at every aspect of your life. You are committed to your obligations both at work and at home seriously, and live an existence that is rooted in your beliefs, values and honesty.

Self-love allows you to let yourself down every now and again. You indulge yourself with treats every now and again and you remember to be happy and be happy in each moment. If you are truly happy with yourself it's much easier to create healthy relationships and to love others, too.

Chapter 3: To Create Inner Peace Using Mindfulness Meditation?

Indulging yourself in stressful and embarrassing circumstances can indicate a the lack of self-love. If you truly care about yourself and are gentle with yourself and your family, you'll take the time to take a breather and unwind. If you are truly in love with yourself you'll try to calm your thoughts, quiet your inner critic, and manage your thoughts.

Mindfulness meditation is a method that is employed by many spiritual mystics to strengthen their brains to relax their minds and their body, and attain peace and tranquility within themselves.

If you don't love yourself, your thoughts are filled with negative and critical thoughts. You continually criticize and despise yourself and think negative thoughts. Meditation is a great way to disarm your inner critic and help promote peace. When you consistently practice mindfulness, you become less critical of yourself. You'll come to know yourself just a more, and you will accept yourself for who you are. Meditation helps you find peace within because it assists you manage your body, your emotions as well as your thoughts. It improves self-awareness, and like we mentioned earlier self-awareness is an vital component of self-love.

Here's how to practice mindfulness meditation to improve your appreciation for yourself

1. Pick a space in your bedroom or your office to sit and meditate, and where you will not be distracted or disturbed.

2. Find a comfortable seat and then close your eyes. Be aware of all the things you touch as well as smell, taste or hear.

3. Deep breaths, inhale through your nose, and exhale with your mouth and allow your rib cage to expand.

4. Keep your eyes in your breath. In your head, you can say "Inhaling" and after that, "Exhaling".

5. If a thought occurs If you think about it, mark your thought "Thinking". Don't judge either yourself, or what you think. Just return your attention and thoughts to your breathing.

6. Keep your attention on the present Do not dwell on your past or fret about your future.

7. Breathe and let go all the negative labels you often give yourself. Let go of all negative thoughts you think you have regarding other people. Get rid of all your negative thoughts about the world as well as yourself. Let it all go.

8. Make a small prayer of gratitude , and slowly take a deep breath and open your eyes.

To benefit from meditation, it is essential to keep practicing it consistently. It's also helpful to keep a steady practice of mindfulness throughout the day, whether you are at work eating, walking, or eating. While eating, you should engage all your senses. Take note of every bite, be attentive as you chew. When you walk across the lot from your parking spot to the office Pay attention to each step. Be aware of the environment around you. Be conscious of what your body does and eats as well as the thoughts that pop to your mind.

If you're conscious of your negative thoughts and emotions and you choose to let them go of them and not judge yourself, you're much better in charge of the life you live, and you can find inner peace. Peace of mind is the greatest gift you can give to yourself.

The Importance of A Daily Routine, and Self Love

The majority of laptop users tweak their computers and check their Facebook accounts at the beginning of the day. They will spend in the beginning 20 mins of the day scouring the internet and checking the status of other people's relationships, vacations clothes, and even family on social networks. The practice may appear innocent at first, but sociologists have repeatedly warned that social media sites could damage self-esteem of users.

One drawback of social media websites is that they encourage users to present an over-exaggerated image of themselves. Many people boast about their satisfaction and perfect relationships on social media sites, when actually, they're trying to make the ends meet. If you're spending a significant amount hours on Facebook or other sites for networking you'll likely to feel dissatisfied with your life as well as your lifestyle. You may feel discontent with how others live their lives. It is easy to compare yourself and your lifestyle to the lives of others. This is a risk because it creates feelings of self-worthlessness as well as discontentment and unhappy.

If you're looking to boost your self-love it is essential to establish your own routine for the morning which will boost confidence in yourself, confidence in yourself, self-esteem and self-love. It can help you do your best in all you do, each and each day.

Here's a morning routine you can perform every day that will ensure you begin your day on the right foot and boost your self-love

* Get up earlier than necessary. It is essential to be up immediately the moment you awake in the early morning. You'll feel exhausted and annoyed if you keep at it with the snooze feature in your alarm clock. Once the alarm sounds you must get up immediately.

* Instead of taking a puff of smoke right upon waking, reach for the glass of water. Drinking water right when you get up will make you feel more energetic and fit. It's also a fantastic way to begin your day.

Make sure to stretch. Stretching can help prepare your body to be ready for the day ahead. It can also help you connect to all the nerves and cells within your body.

* Remind yourself of things you're grateful for. Make time to be grateful for the blessings you have. Make time to be thankful for the small things are often overlooked. Be grateful for your vehicle, your home or your family members, the business you run, as well as even your job. Consider yourself grateful for your family and friends as well as your hardworking colleagues and your generous neighbors.

* Imagine and visualize your goals. Love yourself by allowing you to be a dreamer and having goals. Make time every day to take a seat and think about your ideal future. Imagine the things you would like to have - a big home, luxurious vehicle, a successful career or a profitable business.

* This is the most important steps of your morning routine. take the time to look at yourself in the mirror and tell nice things to yourself. Take note of the things you admire about yourself. Take note of your gorgeous hair beautiful and flawless skin, beautiful eyes and even your stunning mind. Recognize your beauty and accept your imperfections. Be careful not to judge yourself. This is not narcissism however, it is self-acceptance as well as self-love.

Get your day started with a healthy type of breakfast. If you're familiar with the standard Western breakfast of white bread bacon, eggs, bacon and ham, it's time to indulge in greater amounts of fruits and veggies. Instead of having the standard Western breakfast, try smoothies, soup with vegetables or fresh fruits. Breakfast that is healthy is one of the most effective ways to feel loved by yourself.

It is essential to begin your day with a positive attitude, you'll feel more productive and productive. As consequently, you'll feel less anxious and stressed. If you've got an optimistic and healthy morning routine your day will flow smoothly.

Why You Need Self-Discipline to Improve Your Self-Esteem and Love Yourself?

Self-discipline can be identified to be "the ability to manage your emotions and feelings, and to be able to keep pursuing something that is important in spite of the numerous opportunities to give it up". It's the ability to control your behavior as well as your moods and thoughts.

If you are self-motivated and have self-control, then you are able to stand by your values and have the control of your life. Integrity and accountability is an important aspect in self-esteem as well as self-love. If you regularly deviate from the tasks and obligations you have and then go against your beliefs and beliefs, you'll eventually experience frustration and anger with your self. If you consistently choose enjoyable activities over important ones then your life will end up being chaotic and it'll be difficult to attain what you've always thought of. Being self-controlled and disciplined can help you organize your life.

If you consistently say "no" in regards to activities that aren't important or are harmful for you , like drinking excessive alcohol and junk food, smoking cigarettes, too much TV , and spending excessively, you show accountability for your actions and it is an indication of how much you love yourself. If you are constantly saying "no" to things that do not align with your core values like alcoholism, promiscuity and unethical practices at work and even mediocrity, it becomes more easy to be self-confident, and it's much easier to be able to be a person you love.

If you are constantly practicing discipline and self-control Your life will be on the right path. If you are consistently saying "no" to food that is junk and other unhealthy foods you'll be healthy and fit, and it will be more easy to appreciate your body. If you are determined to get up each day to run and exercise to keep your body in great condition. If you always choose to study over socializing, you'll eventually land a great job and be successful in your career. It's easier to feel comfortable and happy with a flourishing job and a balanced lifestyle. If you put in endless hours studying an art, you'll eventually reap the benefits and utilize that skill to lead a better life.

Self-control is an essential component of self-love as well as self-esteem. If you're self-control you'll feel more confident about yourself and the abilities you have. If you're self-disciplined you will live a life you desire and are entitled to. If you're disciplined you are at ease with yourself along with your daily life. The control you have over your life and yourself is the most important element of self-esteem. Self-esteem is the primary ingredient of self-love.

How to stop insecurity for Good and Regain Control Over Your Feelings?

One method to demonstrate self-love is to get rid of and manage all your anxieties and feelings of unworthiness. A lot of experts believe that self-love and self-esteem as well as confidence in yourself are all based on an emotion. Self-confidence and self-esteem are based on the way we perceive ourselves. If you're looking to boost your confidence and self-esteem as well as improve your self-love, you need to alter how you perceive yourself.

To alter your mood and the way you perceive yourself, you must modify your assumptions about yourself and the self-image you have. If you are self-defeating and don't appreciate yourself or love your self-esteem, then you're a victim of an unflattering self-image. One of the primary reasons for low self-esteem and low self-esteem is feeling like you're not good enough. This is an insecurity feeling. This feeling could be connected to your appearance, the level of your education or the wealth that you own. The second belief that has to be changed is our perception or view of what success should be defined.

If you were raised in a family packed with regulations that "should be" then you'll eventually feel that you're not enough unless you're "perfect". This is why those with low self-esteem are typically perfectionists. To get rid of your fears and to feel confident, you must be realistic about the perception you have of your success and the acceptable behaviors. To get rid of your fears and feel confident about yourself, you need to feel proud of your accomplishments.

It is possible that you are not the CEO of a multinational corporation However, you're great in your middle management position and you own a car, an apartment, you have wonderful family members and are able to afford a holiday to a remote island every two or three times a year. You should take a breather and praise God for all the blessings that you enjoy. It's possible that you aren't the same level of smart like Bill Gates and you may not be able solve complex math problems However, you're equipped with the ability to make smart choices and complete your task efficiently. You could paint or play the guitar or even dance. To get rid of your fears and to be confident, you must appreciate your abilities and talents.

The way you perceive yourself is the consequence of the negative beliefs that you've developed through the decades. If you change your self-image and develop positive beliefs about yourself Your self-esteem and confidence will increase and you will feel more confident about yourself.

The health of relationships in Your Life and How They Influence Your Love for Yourself

Our relationships can have a huge impact on our lives , and they certainly have an influence on the affection and love we show to ourselves. Erich Fromm believes that a healthy self-love can be the foundation of all positive relationship. Healthy and happy relationships. You can't love someone else when you don't love yourself first.

If you don't love yourself, you'll have weak boundaries. If you are not careful you will allow the people around you take advantage of you. If you don't love yourself, you depend on external circumstances or other people to make you feel good about your self. If you don't love yourself, you are more likely to accept the poor treatment of your parents, spouse or even your friends as you don't feel you deserve higher standard of treatment.

But, just as your self-love has an effect on the wellbeing of your relationships, the well-being of your relationships impacts your self-love. If you are married to someone who abuses you regularly emotionally and physically and emotionally, your self-esteem will gradually diminish and you'll be conditioned to believe that you do not deserve the abuse and are not worthy of affection.

If the people you cherish regularly ridicule you, you'll have less faith in your own self. If you're engaged to one who is constantly snubbed by your feelings, you'll eventually believe that you are not worthy of the same treatment. Bad relationships can be detrimental to your health. Here are some indications that you're in a bad relationship:

1. Your partner is a bad person and says rude words to you regularly. Your parents,

partner, or even your family members constantly critique you.

2. Your family members and friends aren't taking you seriously and are often unkind to you.

3. It is impossible to grow while you're in a relationship. Your relationship doesn't permit you to grow both personally and professionally.

4. It is as if all your positive energy is taken away out of you.

5. Keep fighting, and you'll always be in conflict.

6. The other person has the power as well as control of you. You aren't sure if you're in charge of you any longer.

7. You are unhappy with yourself.

If you're in a relationship that isn't working You must determine whether it is possible to save or modified. In the event that it is not possible, then it might be the best for your self-esteem to go. The decision to leave a relationship that is not working is among the most effective ways to show compassion and love to yourself.

The importance of goals in regards to Self-Love and Confidence

If you set goals and strive to reach the goals you set, then you will increase the likelihood of achieving success in your life. If you are consistently successful in your endeavors you will feel more confident in yourself and you'll come to like and cherish yourself more.

Setting goals is among the most effective ways to boost self-love and increase confidence in your self. While self-love and self-confidence are largely based on perception but you should not overlook the fact that accomplishment and success can be a powerful way to boost self-confidence and self-love. Achieving goals and goals in life can instantly increase your self-esteem and confidence.

But what exactly is an objective? The majority of people believe that they have goals in their life. They will always claim that their aim is to own the luxury of a Jaguar and a home with 10 bedrooms and a lot of money in their account. But, According to coaches for life, they aren't objectives, they are just dreams and desires which are common to the majority of people. Goals are something that has been carefully planned and is constantly evolving as time passes.

A goal can be described as a planned vision or desired outcome that an individual is obligated to attain. It isn't much of a goal however, it's something that has a similar aim and the goal. If you've set a goal that you're working towards, you'll have a solid sense of purpose . A conviction to achieve it is among the strongest ways to build self-confidence as well as self-esteem.

20 Tips To Set The Perfect Goals

As we have discussed Goals aren't just desires. They are a systematic process and provide us with a sense of direction and purpose. It is essential to set objectives in life. However, for a happy and fulfilled life, it's crucial to establish the correct goals.

Here are a few guidelines that are required when making the right objectives:

1. Set goals that bring you joy As children, we believe that there's a specific model of the goals we should pursue. When we were children we were taught to seek out more money, a bigger home, diamonds, and even a fancy car But is that really your ultimate goal? Do you think it will make you feel happy? Researchers and psychologists have concluded that happiness is the first step to the achievement. People who are content with their lives and what they work for are usually successful, not just at work but also throughout their lives.

2. Create Intrinsic Goals - As mentioned previously, we often get caught in the mistake of thinking that we have to be successful line with the social norms of what success looks like. The society wants us to pursue the pursuit of beauty, money, and fame. The intrinsic goals are those that make us feel content. These goals allow us to improve as individuals. Inspiring goals can help you achieve your personal

development or to make a lasting contribution to society.

3. Make goals that are akin to Your Values Find out what is most important to you. Check that your goals aren't at odds with your values and the values you believe in.

4. Review your life. Before setting an objective, you need examine your current life. What do you believe is not working? What are the aspects of your life you'd like to change or enhanced?

5. Make a deadline. Goals without a timeframe is simply unattainable. A deadline can motivate you to put in more effort to reach your target.

6. Realistic - You must create a plan that is achievable and realistic. That's not to say that you should not set your sights for the sky. If you want to earn 1 million dollars over the course of one year or even 2 years could be feasible however making 1 million dollars in one month isn't realistic, especially if you've never made anything close to one million dollars prior to.

7. Set positive goals and structure your goals using positive words. In place the phrase "Do avoid being late" choose "Be on time". Positive affirmations are more motivating.

8. Determine your priorities. When you're setting goals you must determine what your top priorities are. Your goals must be in line with your goals.

9. The goal must be precise The goal must be specific. It is essential to state the date and time it must occur. It is essential to specify the goals you intend to achieve. The goal that states "I would like to be wealthy" is usually not very successful. It is important to be clear regarding the amount you'd like and when you'd like to achieve it, and the strategies you'll utilize to attain it.

10. The goal must be measurable . You should be able measure your objectives as this will inspire you to put in a lot of effort to accomplish it. If your goals can be measured then you'll know whether you're making advancement.

11. Select a model or idea - If you're hoping to build your own company or become successful in your career, you must examine the success of those who accomplished it. What were their objectives and how did they accomplish those objectives?

12. If you've accomplished your goal, you can choose an even more difficult and thrilling target - Your goals must be both challenging and thrilling. Some people select goals they are able to easily accomplish. If you select an ambitious goal, you'll feel more content once you've completed it.

13. Make a list of your objectives Your goals will not be able to hold any weight unless you put them down on the paper. When you record those goals they are tangible and you're more determined to strive to reach your goals.

14. Imagine - Take the time to consider your goals and imagine what it feels to reach your goals. Imagine your life between two and five years from today. Are you able to achieve your goals? What is it like living your life you've always wanted? How do you feel when you achieve success? It is also

possible to create your own vision board, where you can put up images that symbolize your dreams and goals. life.

15. Reduce your goals into smaller pieces If you have large goals, it's best to break that big goal into smaller goals. This means that your goal will be much easier to accomplish and you are able to be grateful for small victories and progress toward your larger goals.

16. Brainstorming - While goals should be individual, it's ideal to discuss your ideas with those who can help you set fantastic goals. It is possible to think about your goals with your spouse, friends sisters, or an expert in life coaching.

17. Set your goals in writing After you have established your goals, it is important to announce your goals publicly. This is a highly effective method for setting goals for a lot of people. The act of putting your goals out there will make you more committed to reach these goals.

18. Develop a strategy - Don't make goals and set them but you must develop an

extensive strategic plan for how to achieve them. If you've got a clear plan, it's much simpler to accomplish your objectives.

19. Choose a goal-setting buddy Find a goal partner who will assist you in reviewing your goals and keep track of your progress. Your goal-setting buddy will help you and encourage you while you strive to reach your goals.

20. Set your sights on your goals After you've set your goals, you need to commit fully to reaching it.

They are essential and, while the goal behind setting the goal is to reach it but you will also be rewarded with lessons, experiences and advancements throughout the course. If you set a goal then your life will be in an obvious direction. You're in charge of your life, and you are in charge of your own life.

How to Measure Your Progress and Reward Yourself Everyday For Falling in Love with Yourself and Building confidence

To increase your love for yourself, you need be able to keep track of your progress on a regular basis. Here's how to keep track of your improvements:

1. Make a list of the tasks you have to complete in order to demonstrate and practice self-love. The list looks like this:

• Breakup with my abusive girlfriend or boyfriend.

* Send nice thoughts to me.

* Check in your mirror every morning to appreciate my gorgeous appearance.

Appreciate the blessings I've received.

* Set goals.

• Follow through to my objectives.

* Remind yourself to visualize and affirm each day.

* Do at least thirty minutes per day.

* Get more vegetables and fruits.

* Visit places that I haven't been to before.

Take on bullies.

* Dress to impress.

• Get a manicure each week.

2. Each task should be written on the calendar. Print an agenda to each job. Each day, write down the date on the calendar if you're competent to complete the task. This will allow you to track your progress and keep track of your consistency.

3. Pay attention to the changes that you notice in the relationships. If you show self-love regularly and are respected by others, they will love you more.

4. Be aware of the changes that have occurred in your work. If you are more in love with yourself then your career will prosper and you'll become much more effective in your field of work.

5. Create a weekly or monthly personal review. It's similar to the quarterly reviews you receive at work. Make sure to take the time to look over your progress and evaluate what strategies are working and which ones aren't effective.

If you've made progress and your feelings for yourself has increased, then be sure to reward yourself for doing loving acts for yourself. You could go to spa treatments, indulge in the most delicious ice cream in town, or go out for dinner at a restaurant that is expensive. You can also purchase new clothing and shoes. Finally, you should make sure to pat yourself on the back. You deserve it!

Chapter 4: Everyone Is Hurt

There were many times during my life that I was afraid that I was not good enough. I believed that I was not worthy of to the world, and I'd never be accepted. As a young person I had a lot of trouble trying to be social and didn't have any friends until seventeen. At the very least I did have some "frenemies" as I were younger but there were always frictions and issues. If you've read my book on depression, then you are aware that I was faced with a variety of emotional issues in my younger years. However, in this book we will take it a step further.

We will discuss the ways in which we interact with others. If you're like me, then you've suffered a lot of hurt throughout your life. You've heard people speak words that cause pain. As a kid, everyone's been told over and over, "Sticks and stones may cause me to break bones but words will never harm me," and, "I'm rubber, you're glue. Whatever that you speak bounces off my back and sticks to me." These are tiny phrases to disguise how much words from people's mouths can cause harm. However, it's not only the words of others; often I'm also my own worst critic. I glance at myself in the mirror and I'm not pleased with my reflection. I am constantly questioning my abilities in the field of writing, teacher, businessman and an entrepreneur constantly. Sometimes, I am unsure whether I'm a good enough father.

The thoughts are bouncing around in my mind. I'd like to be completely transparent with you in this memoir. I believe that leadership starts from the front. I'll share some extremely personal aspects of myself to help you feel more at ease with your own personal disappointments. Sometimes, I look at my children and ask myself, "Am I already behind?" My daughter is four years old. She is only able to speak three languages. Would I have been better? Could I've done something else? My son is just 15 months old and cannot swim without flotation devices. Why is he unable to swim without floaties?

If you are familiar with a little about swimming and languages it is clear that both my kids are extremely advanced, yet these thoughts can worm through my mind occasionally. It is because the majority of our opinions about ourselves do not come from the facts or logic and are in fact harmful thoughts that are floating around within our minds. These are merely whispers. They're made to harm you rather than to help you learn. The little babbling thoughts you have won't assist me as father. They restrict me.

The book we're going to address this issue all together. Actually, we're going to do more than this and I am thrilled. The book is more than learning how to love yourself. It's about teaching everyone else to be into love with yourself as well. And we'll assist you in developing impressive capabilities and assets. We will help you improve your self-confidence as well as self-esteem and charisma. These are some lofty goals, but I love to take on big goals.

Try to aim for the stars, and, if you don't succeed you'll miss the moon. What do you think? Nobody has been on the moon in since the 1970s. The time is now to take it. We've stopped shooting for stars. In spite of all the talk about colonizing Mars I'd rather take an excursion into the lunar surface. I'd love to see how the moon's appearance is in HD and I'd like to see iPhone images from the moon. Does the iPhone operate in an empty space? I'd love to know. I don't believe it requires oxygen, but maybe all Apple products require oxygen for breathing.

I'd like you to consider in the same way about yourself.

Let's set some wild goals. Let's achieve things Let's turn you into an extremely confident and successful superstar who is self-confident. Let's go further and make you more charismatic. Charisma is when you say things and people are excited. They are drawn by your magnetic persona is a force of gravity.

Personality Skills: What are They, and Why are They Essential?

While we work through this book, we're going to be doing a lot of fun things together, and we'll begin by assessing the current situation. It is important to know what you're about and look into your motivations and emotions. What we'll analyze is your intrapersonal abilities.

The ability of your intrapersonal skills is to assess and measure yourself, to analyze your mood as well as your motivation, mental state and living. It's the ability to examine yourself and say, "I'm depressed," "I'm not depressed,"" "I'm content," "I'm not happy." There's no instrument that a physician could use to gauge your happiness level even if you're not speaking. This is the reason why a psychiatrist's biggest fear is someone who isn't talking; they aren't aware of the cause and they have nothing that they could do to assist. Like gravity, psychologists are able to analyze the impact of your emotions, however they can't observe them in person. They are able to observe the way your emotions impact the way you speak, and how your words can tell them the story of what's happening.

This book is about self-awareness as well as self-management. Self-awareness is knowing and managing yourself is managing the process. When you finish this book, you're going to be in total control over the business. We will fire all the bad middle managers who have been wrecking your business's emotional health for way too long.

Let's examine the examples of interpersonal skills As you look at your own self-worth, I would like you to consider your position on the range. It's worth writing your responses into the Love Yourself Journal.

1. Do you have an in-depth knowledge of your own thinking motives and processes? Do you know the reason you choose to do certain things? If there is a time when that you feel sad Are you aware of the reason you are feeling sad? If your sadness is over do you know the reason why it ended? And what led to it ending? Do you feel as if you are in the sea, being tossed around by the whirlwind of emotions and the winds of nature? Do you know what the winds are coming from?

2. Do you keep track of your thoughts and your motivations? Do you actively resist

negativity? This is the most important step. This is an act of self-management. If you start to notice that you are becoming distressed, angry, or confused Do you do something about it? Are you like my father and me when we're lost, and we don't not do anything but ask for directions? Do you accept the negative thing that is taking place and sit back and wait until the storm is over? pass?

3. Do you try to avoid negative and destructive thoughts? Sometimes, we experience physical triggers. One example of my negative thoughts is that I am a sucker for snack, and I'm unable to stop myself from eating certain actions. If you've seen images of me, or read the negative messages I receive my weight is usually the focus of these discussions. If there's food in my home I am not equipped with the capability of avoiding it. I know this. That's why there aren't any snacks in my home. There's not one chip bag, and there aren't any cookie tins. All the things I find myself craving are present. My entire family is slim My wife and my children are healthy and fit. A large part of it is because my children are

her children and another reason is due to the fact that they share my fear of suffering the same issues with weight that my own experience has.

When I see the negative thoughts that is trying to enter my mind I immediately take action to restrain. Do you experience the same thing? If you are beginning to notice that you are becoming obese and depressed, will you act? If you've have read my book on depression, then you are aware that whenever depression strikes I always tell someone and then do something exciting to combat it. If you've gone through Overcoming Depression and are taking steps, then declare "yes" to the suggestions here. But if you're one who let the negativity be a part of your life and let it take over the situation, you're stuck with "no."

4. Have you got the capacity to think clearly? Do you have the capacity to envision the goal, desire or something you'd like before you? Do you remain there for long enough to influence you? Do you find that these visualizations appear like a flash

in the pan? Are they an ephemeral memory of ghosts?

5. Are you adept at internal decisions and problem-solving? Can you identify the root of a problem and implement a solution to correct the situation? Do you recognize that you are a victim of negative patterns, behaviors or thought process and then find an answer?

6. What would you say about your self on a scale from 1-10 on the scale of mindfulness? Mindfulness is the capacity to be present and concentrate on only the "right moment." It's when you do not think about yesterday and don't worry about tomorrow or regret your previous decisions and do not worry about what is to follow. Your mind is too busy living.

Another way to be mindful is observing the way people utilize technology. I don't really take lots of photos these days; in fact, I must take a conscious decision to take my camera. There are so many cameras in my home and every phone within the home has cameras. We're a very camera-loving family, yet this isn't how I want to live. I do not want be living life through a camera. I'd rather be with my family in this moment. I'd rather watch my child take a dip and then embrace him instead of taking a thousand photos of the water. Are you living in the present? Are you stuck within the past? Do you see life through technology?

7. Do you try to avoid thinking and actions? One counterproductive thing to do is to purchase snacks and then put them in the kitchen which I would be fighting against myself. It's like having landmines in your home; avoid this. You may make choices that can tempt you. If you're a person who has a problem to drink, then a harmful behaviour is to say, "I could just have one." This is the most frequent remark of a who relapses. There will be no problem; it's not a big problem. This is a condition I've had to deal in my family. I know about the effects because I've had to deal with it often. Are you constantly thinking about things that you already know are harmful to you?

8. Do you have the capacity to think in depth? Do you feel stuck in the surface? An effective way to find out how deep you

think is to take a look at what people say when you talk to someone. Do you ever wander your mind to ask what they were thinking?

There's a classic scene from an old film that is repeated many times because it's hilarious; one person must get rid of their pet, and they make up a story about how they be mad at the dog in order to convince it to go away. The dog is unhappy and the dog shouts and yells and is forced to throw a rock and eventually, the dog goes away. When you look at the surface of the situation you might consider, "Wow, that kid dislikes the dog." However, when you know the background of the situation and looked further, you'd be able to understand the motivation that drove the decision. It could be that his neighbor was about to take his dog's life, and the dog's owner had to conceal the dog to protect the life of it or some other reason.

Do you ever consider what is the "why" behind what people are saying to you?

Think about these issues and then start taking action here. Get your notebook. I would like you to name it the Love Yourself Journal. If you're super tech-savvy it might be a good idea to create this on your tablet or another device that is on your phone. But I prefer to do this manually. What we're dealing with this time is an emotional issue. All of these worries anxieties, stress and tensions are in your mind. Insecurity and lack of charisma happen inside your mind. We must address these issues in the place where they are most vulnerable in the outside of your body.

Making it happen through physical action can be more motivating. More "in reality" your solution is, the simpler the process will be. Note down your responses to these questions. Analyzing your personal abilities will allow you to know what you're doing right now. You can go through the exercises within Your Love Yourself Journal, and when you're done, you'll have a written account of how you started and where you came to.

Intrapersonal Intelligence Test

We've examined a number of big picture issues and we're going to get into the details. We began with the forest, now we will examine the trees. I've put together a few very specific questions that you need to consider. Let's evaluate your current inner-personal intelligence level.

1. How well do you do being by yourself? Do you love your private company?

A) I enjoy being with my friends, and I like being by myself occasionally.

B) I struggle to be by myself.

2. Are you adept at keeping on top of your thinking and deflecting negative thinking?

A) I'm quite proficient at this.

B) The majority of the time.

3. In general, how powerful are you at controlling your thoughts?

A) Very strong or strong.

B) Not particularly powerful or solid.

4. If you experience negative thoughts concerning yourself, what adept do you manage to dismiss these feelings and taking

a positive path instead? Also how proficient do you have at being nice to yourself?

A) Very good or excellent.

B) Not the best.

Score: The more "A" responses you select the more advanced your intrapersonal abilities are. If you picked lots of "b" answers Don't fret! All of us are capable of developing our personal skills.

Note the score you scored within the Love Yourself Journal. It is important to keep the score, because as we progress and improve it, we'll be able to increase it. Whatever level you're currently, we'll be there to help you improve. By the close of this book we will assist you in getting better.

Questions for Reflection

What I'd like you do is think about the following five questions , and include your responses in the Love Yourself Journal. Through these questions, you should try to get in touch with your most profound thoughts.

1. What do you know about yourself at the moment? What steps do plan to take to know yourself a more?

2. What are your top three characteristics?

3. Right now, do you love yourself? Tell me honestly You can answer this question with a"yes or "no"; or perhaps you should give yourself a scale, for instance, you are loving yourself 87 percent. However, here's a question: how do you think this will go in the event that I tell my wife I love her by eighty-seven percent?

If the answer you're getting right today"no" right now, then "no," look in an mirror or in your own soul and ask yourself "Why you don't?" What is holding you back? There may be actions you've made in the past, or made decisions you regret. The past holds a grip on you. Maybe you're not the way you'd like to be and you're looking at the future and you're not exactly what you'd like it be. Examine it and determine what's wrong. Does it have to do with your character? Do you have people that surround you? What's missing?

4. On a scale from 1 up to 10, what would you evaluate your self-confidence and confidence? What do you think of in yourself? How do you feel you are confident in your capacity to act? Do you believe that you can be able to effectively face the challenges and issues that life throws at you?

5. Do you think that you are able an eminent person? Why or why you don't? On an scale of 1-10 evaluate your charm.

6. For a final thought If you were to conclude, do you think increasing your self-confidence and self-esteem could bring about an improvement in your self-confidence?

Talking to Yourself

Do you now have a clear understanding of what we're going to tackle in this book, and the value of intrapersonal abilities. You might be thinking about how to build these abilities; how can people improve their personalities? These are important questions since they form the basis of the journey we're embarking on together.

For an enjoyable and satisfying life, having strong intrapersonal abilities are essential. A lot of people believe that skills in the intrapersonal realm are an ability that you're born with. or either way, or you do not. However, a skill is an acquired and strengthened skill which we can enhance. This is an extremely important distinction.

When I was younger, there were many areas in my life that I had weaknesses I believed that they were weaknesses. I thought that I was born with a great or bad personality, famous or not either happy or unhappy. I believed that there was no way to change this, and I was a complete misunderstanding. Anyone is able to decide to develop their thoughts or their inner-personal abilities. It's all it takes is a bit of effort and reflection however, the effort are worth it.

When you improve your thinking life, when you are your own most fervent fan and then become in love with yourself once more You will experience some incredible outcomes, such as greater self-awareness and a higher confidence in your mental wellbeing and a greater confidence in your life, more confidence, an increased degree of self-love and others, a real feeling of wisdom, deeper understanding, a greater awareness of your own abilities and the ability to communicate with others.

Before we can enjoy excellent communication and strong relationships with others before we are able to form emotional bonds and connect with others, we need to be able to comprehend and love ourselves. This is the first step to success.

Techniques to Increase Your Personal Awareness

Like any other area we'd like to grow in and improve, I'd like to offer you a variety of tools and strategies that you can employ. I've got an extensive list of techniques you can apply to increase your personal skills. you'll find some the methods easy while others are more difficult. You must step outside your familiar zone. Don't expect to apply all of these techniques every day throughout your life. This isn't the way we can achieve success. What we are looking for is the methods that are successful for you, the methods that you like and that you have satisfaction with, and you are able to implement over time.

What I would like to request is that you test every one of these methods at least two times. There are times when you have a negative experience when you first try something new, so I suggest you to do it again to make sure that we have the most effective techniques for you. When we go through these techniques you'll find the most effective personal mix of strategies to provide yourself with the insight you've always wanted to know.

1. Regular meditation

Self-awareness is among the crucial steps along this road. The best way to become conscious is to shut off our thoughts that are primarily focused on the surface for a short time and allow our other brains the chance to go deeply and find out what's happening. There are a lot of preconceived notions regarding meditation, but I'd ask to let them go and try it. Meditation isn't about emptying your thoughts and leaving you exposed to random thoughts; it's quite the opposite. Meditation is all about removing negative thoughts about the past as well as the future.

We tend to spend the majority of our time thinking about things that we cannot change, or things that are unlikely to occur. If you are in the state of meditation it is possible to remove the unnecessary aspects and concentrate on the matters that are important. You are more in tune with your inner feelings and what's happening at the moment. It's not necessary to do any specific form practice or repeat a specific phrase. It can be as simple as laying down, putting aside any distractions and focusing only on the body.

Begin by sitting in a still position and taking note of your breathing. Take note of the way that breath flows into and out of your lung. Reduce your pace and be in control over your breath. This is an action is so routine and we view it as a natural process, similar to the heartbeat, however in reality, you hold control over your breathing. You can take a few minutes to take the control of your body, and take note of how that feels. Don't think about the past, and don't focus on the future; simply think about how to complete this task properly. Focus all your focus to doing something that is right. At that point you will realize that all is well; you will feel the first signs of consciousness. While in that state you'll observe the mental clutter starts to fade away; you will be able to better assess your thoughts and feelings about the world around you. it is that you really feel about things.

Meditation can help you begin the process of gaining control over your mind. In the West we often assign special power to emotions. Our culture, certain medical professionals, and the majority of media view emotions as magic powers that be completely controlled like emotions can cause you to behave like a puppet string. These are powerful legal arguments, but they're only illusions and smoke. You have control over your feelings. They are just thoughts. Regaining control over your mind and asserting your power starts by focusing on your thoughts.

2. Keep a Personal Reflective Journal

Perhaps, you've already created your Love Yourself Journal, where you'll be writing down your answers to test questions, your reflective thoughts, as well as your experiences through the journey. Even after you've finished this book, you must not stop writing down the way you feel about things. We're not very good in recollecting the experiences we have. When I inquire one month from today how you felt today There's a 99.99 percent chance that you won't recall, unless you record it down.

Everyone has revisionist memories that alter how we view things as we age Our memories also change. Only way you can ensure you have an a precise document of your experience is to record it in a journal. We need to be able to control what you recall about your past experiences, so that you can keep track of your progress. Journaling has assisted me in various procedures. I've been through times when, after six months of transformation, I feel as if I'm being a complete failure. However, I look back at the very beginning of my journey and see that I'm at a place that I had never imagined I could be able to achieve.

Things I'd never dreamed of accomplishing have turned into my down times, and when I think about my past I am able to observe my path since I recorded it. Instead of thinking that you've got evidence that you've made it up an incline and are doing incredible things.

Sometimes, we feel insignificant within our society and feel that our actions aren't affecting any result, and that we aren't able to change the course that our actions have on our future. Noting down your experiences, your feelings and the things that you do will make you aware that you are in control. You'll experience a greater sense of control, and your life will be in sync with your mental life. If you're feeling like you're not efficient, your self-confidence is not positive, and you're not sure of how to be truly happy with yourself It is likely that you're not in a state of congruity. Congruity is when your inner life and the outside as well as your mind and body, are aligned. The higher your level of congruity is, the more difficult your mental barriers get. It is only possible to develop this ability when we fully know what's going on and are in good shape.

The goal of keeping journals isn't for it to turn into homework or to add stress to your life. The majority of people are not happy with the beginning of their journaling, but one month later it is a crucial element of your life that you cannot think of not doing. Journaling becomes a part of your life that you are thrilled about. You'll need to put in some effort initially and then it will develop its own rhythm and then it is something you look forward toand observe how you've performed. It's like looking at the world as a scoring board and you're excited to see the achievements you've done each day.

3. Improve Your Self-Esteem

There are many things we do in our day-to-day lives that make us feel uncomfortable. There are those who believe that the glass is half-full, others think that the glass is half empty There are those who make fun about it and attempt to come up with a third solution. The goal is to gauge your self-talk and see where you fall between optimism to pessimism. Many people excuse their optimism and negative thinking patterns by claiming it's realism however it's not.

If you have trouble with this issue, you could use to use the Love Yourself Journal to be efficient: every moment you are faced with thoughts of something negative that could happen Write it down. In the course of a few weeks, take a look at the predictions your brain made and note those that were to pass. You'll discover the brain's completely ineffective in predicting the future. Ninety-nine percent of the times you'll be right and you'll discover that pessimism isn't real in any way. Be grateful and allow yourself to be content with your achievements. If you have achieved something, you should celebrate the accomplishment, no matter the size of it.

When you can celebrate small steps and you are happy with the process. If you're allowed to celebrate once you have completed something, or if you choose to only be happy when you've finished reading the entire book, then you'll most likely be unsuccessful, or at the very least you won't be able to appreciate the process. If you set up artificial expectations, you'll never be successful. Be grateful for the tiny steps, and you'll soon be making your brain more enthused about the process. If each time you mess into focusing on failure instead of the achievement, you associate a negative feeling to the attempt. You teach yourself not to make a mistake, but if claim that you've done your best , then you'll be better the next time.

If you are acting for yourself like the great friend in the gym who assists you in lifting your weights or that boxer's pal in the corner, who shouts, "You can do it champ, just one more time and you'll have the man!" then you can be your own greatest fan, your personal biggest fan. Start to get rid of self-talk that is negative, and stop talking about things like "I'm useless," "I'm a loser," "I'm useless," "I am a failure forever." The negative self-talk aren't going to anything; they're empty words. When you realize that you are making one of these statements you should make a note "Stop! I'm no longer doing that. I'm not useless."

4. Spend more time with people That Make You Feel Happy About You

I've met some individuals in my past that caused me to feel self-conscious about myself. Sometimes, it's because they are bullies. And when we're younger, we encounter this a lot. There are those who try to push us to make themselves feel good, however, sometimes we're in a group of those who cause us to feel uncomfortable due to their low self-esteem.

Misery is a social butterfly and loves to bring you down. If there are individuals in your life who would like to be competitive with you and want to stop you from getting near the sun take some time with them. If you spend a lot of time with someone who is like that, you will lose your self-esteem and also your perception of real life. This person could be in control of your life, and we don't wish for this to happen.

You can change the kind of people that you spend time with and you'll transform your outlook on life. If you are with people who are constantly content, you will be happy every day. They can bring you to their emotional levels. We will be influenced by those we spend the most time with Therefore, why not surround yourself with people whom you really desire to emulate?

5. Do Yourself A favor

It is important to remain on your own and be rewarded when you accomplish something well. It's not about eating an ice cream, pie or cake each whenever you achieve something however it is rewarding yourself with an acknowledgement or a sticker or a chance to feel happy and be happy - however you choose to reward you based on your circumstances. Include healthy rewards in places that will encourage you to achieve your goals. Within Your Love Yourself Journal, if you've got the one I created specifically for you, find there are spaces on each page to add stickers that give you some encouragement. There is nothing more that makes a journal entertaining than a few stickers.

6. Create a Plan for Your Personal development

Through this book, I'll be able offer you strategies, tools and a plan to plan for your future. However, you need to begin taking action now. Begin to think about the things you want to achieve and where you'd like to end up in the next six three months, and even in three weeks. Make sure you set specific, measurable, and achievable goals, create an action plan, and then say, "This is what I will be like within six months. I will no longer have negative thoughts. I would like to be attractive, and I'll have three new friends who will be awed by me."

Be specific and bold Be specific and be bold; dream of large things and they will happen. If you follow through with your plan and achieve the results you wanted Your self-control will be through the roof as you have achieved the target. It turns out that you are able to plan and achieve amazing things.

8. Find some quiet time in Your Life

It could be that is more than just meditation. When we're low on the self-confidence scale We do all we could to fill our lives with sound because we're scared of thoughts that are that are in our heads. I used to lead in a noisy life. I would go to sleep listening to music and I watched TV at all times and be with people as I was scared to be by myself. I was scared of the voices that were in my mind and the negative things they would say about me.

We are moving past the present, and are beginning to gain control over our thoughts to ensure that each day you enjoy a peaceful time. Simply look over your day and take a few moments to take a breath. You're constantly doing; take a moment to look back at your experiences. Connect with yourself and take note of the messages your body and brain are saying to you.

9. Create a reward ritual

Rituals are extremely powerful and can assist us get into various states of mind. I employ rituals in all aspects that I live. I begin every day with a routine to put me at a high level to work, and then when I'm getting ready to write, I use a pre-writing ritual to clear my mind of any distractions and concentrate on writing. it allows me to become extremely fast and proficient when it comes to my words. Being in the right emotional state through rituals can help me become an improved writer. it also helps you get into an optimistic, self-confidence-building state.

The ritual could include getting a massages or creating the process of watching your preferred show. Many people, particularly groups of people who are passionate about an individual show, have a complete ritual to watch it. They gather with their pals on a Saturday evening, and everyone brings food. The host ensures that drinks are served and then everyone gathers to watch the program together and then talk about it afterwards. It's a way to celebrate TV shows, which might be something you've completed, but you're aware of this concept.

Create the same kind of routine within your life. Develop routines that are solely about being with your loved ones and feeling great. It could be as simple as engaging in an activity you love by yourself or with friends, it could be a physical exercise or a mental one.

Certain activities are very cathartic for me since they give me feelings of calm with myself. I've always struggled with exercising but I still enjoy surfing, stand-up paddling and kayaking. When I am feeling stressed out from my day, I'll bring my children to swim in the pool. I'm so occupied with them, they demand 100% focus that I don't have time to think of anything else. their security is at stake and they require all of my attention. It helps me relax, as well as I feel it extremely enjoyable. I enjoy swimming with my kids each day and it helps me stay in a constant state of peace and tranquility. It's a good feeling.

10. Set Goals and Make Follow-up on They

It is important to have experience in completing things. While we're discussing the mental process, it's not like we wish to fight against our mental disorders in areas where they are strong, we'd rather fight them in areas where they are weak. We'd like to combat these issues in real life as well as in the world beyond your body. It's effortless to feel happy when you have achieved something.

Instead of taking you through a variety of mental exercises which make you feel great, let's get things done that make you feel great as you've completed them. The proof is in the pudding There is no reason that doubt will ever enter your mind since with an objective, it's an "yes or no" at the end. You either didn't or you did it.

Set both long-term and short-term goals for both the short and long term. We often set massive, broad New Year's resolutions we never accomplish because they're so far from us. "I would like to shed the weight of 174 pounds." This can take around two or three years, it's just too difficult. Many individuals fail due to the fact that they look to far off that they are out of sight; they can't discern it any more.

If you make ten small goals for the day You'll probably accomplish the entire 10. Begin by breaking down your goals down into chunks that you are able to accomplish. I have small goals I strive to meet each day. I strive to train for an hour each day, go swimming with my kids at least once every day, and release every weekday a podcast episode and the list goes on. I have a blend of work, health, and family goals. Begin small, and then work toward larger goals which will help your self-confidence get stronger and more confident. We are educating ourselves about confidence in ourselves, and training your brain to change the way it thinks.

11. Write your autobiography

If you think your life isn't interesting enough let me assure to you as a professional writer and ghostwriter, whenever people discover what I do for my livelihood, they inform me of the project they're working on. The sheer number of people with terrible lives writing autobiographies and biographies tells me that no matter where you are in your life, you're allowed to write.

The goal of this exercise isn't to make you millionaire or be the most popular writer of all time but to get started to think of your life as an achievement. When you write an autobiography, you are focusing on the highlights of your life and begin to think about and look at what you've achieved through your life. You doubt your own worth since you've forgotten the majority of your greatest achievements. You must quit underestimating yourself. Your journey could be inspiring for others.

When I first began making books to write, my primary goal for the very first novel was to sell 10 copies. If 10 people purchase the novel and listen to my tale, I could have impacted the world. I had my first taste of what was important. After I sold ten units, I was enticed to sell one hundred and after that one thousand. The most important thing most is how you impact the lives of someone. The first time you receive an email from someone who says, "You changed my life," "You motivate me," "You give me the courage to believe again,"" "You have made me more enthusiastic about my living my life." These are the ones you'd like to hear. They can make you feel great and are my most favorite phrases to listen to. In fact, I am looking at you emailing me when you've finished the book to let me know that you're starting to love you all over again.

It is a relaxing and inspiring process that can aid in connecting to your own self. It's exciting to write your story and I'll be reading it. I'll be the first to go through it and provide you with a first review. I'm happy to do it.

12. Discover inspirational Biographies

Discover stories from the real world that you can relate to as well as that inspire and motivate you. The book that I will always will always remember was the 800-page autobiography of the General George Patton. One of the most incredible books I've ever read, and I have read every day a different book!

If you're reading a book and you realize that the protagonist has an opportunity to fail and fail, you are aware of the chance that things could be a disaster and there's a real stake. This is what makes books fascinating for me because it is real. If you decide to read an autobiography, and you know how it's going to end however, the stakes are real , because in the present the moment that things happen and negative scenarios exist. My first novel that has been a success under the name of my own is Serve No Master. This is the name I use for my company, website as well as the majority of my work. It's an autobiography and that's the reason people love it; It is full of highs and lows, as well as the failures and difficulties.

If you'd like to go through the book, you're willing to do it but the point of this book isn't to convince you to purchase other books by me.

Find stories that motivate you. Find a real person who can become your hero. I am listening to a podcast that features an author on television whose views are opposed to; the things he says and thinks I do not agree with, however, what I do appreciate that the fact that he is obsessed by Abraham Lincoln. Lincoln is his top president, and regardless of whether or you are in agreement with someone's opinions, I love it when they are extremely knowledgeable and passionate about certain things.

Find historical figures who are inspiring to you. I find Patton an inspiration, and I'm able to share a myriad of stories about his life. Patton was so skilled in winning that the generals around him were frightened. The British were furious as they were hoping to take over Paris as well as Berlin and were also in discussions about Patton's boss. Patton was the second in command responsible for Third Army. They told them, "You have got to put an end to this guy, He is winning way too many." It would be great be thrilled to hear that people would say the same about me! "Give everyone time to catch up, you're making more than you can handle!"

They could not get him to stop. He was constantly telling them, "I interpreted your orders to take on more territory, and I took it. Forty-four cities have been taken over in the past week. Sorry, I'm not able to slow down being caught in the heat of combat. You can't quit fighting, you can't quit, and must continue beating." The general was an incredible general, however, he also made plenty of mistakes in their attempts to transform him into an official within North Africa. (Special note that I am writing a story in collaboration with one of the Patton's tankers!)

Patton is a famous historical character who inspires me. You must find your favorite. Patton isn't the only one I admire and he's not by any means one of the historical figures I love but it's one I love reading and speaking about. Find stories with actual stakes, and you'll feel the difference.

Questions for Reflection

Inside the Love Yourself Journal, write down your answer to each of the questions below:

1. Which of the methods in the previous section did you like? What ones are you most eager to try and what ones are you currently using in your own life? Perhaps you're already taking actions but didn't know the benefits they could bring to you.

2. What new method do you want to test first?

3. How much room for improvement do you see ahead of you in terms of your intrapersonal capabilities?

Exercise

In the coming two weeks, you'll be able to apply at minimum five of the strategies in this chapter. I suggest you avoid going into Chapter 2 until you've worked through this exercise. You must have recorded the strategies you're planning to test within the Love Yourself Journal, and you should set aside 14 days to try this exercise and then respond to these questions:

1. Do you think you're experiencing more self-awareness?

2. Define how your self-awareness been improved.

3. What could you have done differently in the last two weeks?

4. What do you plan to do in the near future to ensure that your self-awareness grows and get better?

5. Do you feel that your control over your thoughts is greater?

6. What do you think of your belief that your life has improved or increased in the last two weeks?

7. How do you plan to continue to grow and improve in this particular area?

8. Do you believe that you have the ability to manage and control your thoughts? Give a reason why or the reasons why you don't? What are your plans to keep your progress in this field?

Chapter 5: The Mountain Of Wisdom

"Wisdom" is a term that is often used to refer to "smart," "intelligent" or "knowledgeable" however, that's not the purpose of the term. There are many people who are well-versed in things, but have no insight. In my younger years, I believed that people who were older had wisdom. I was of the opinion that you automatically gained wisdom as you the passage of time. As I've gotten older I've learned that there are many older people than me who make poor choices, and the most important thing I do not would like to do is seek the advice of them. I don't wish for my life to play into the same way as theirs.

There are many people in my age group whose lives have taken a turn in directions which I would not like my life to be in. When I think about my friends and family members who have offered me guidance, many have failed to deliver and, if I had followed their suggestions, my life could be much worse. There were some who gave me advice that was sound and I would have loved it if I took it. They were able to impart a little wisdom.

Let's think about our definition of wisdom and what it signifies. Before we can reach the level of wisdom, we must ensure that we know the definition. We can begin by the exercise of brainstorming.

Brainstorming Exercise: What is our definition of Wisdom

Open your Love Yourself Journal. If you own your officially licensed Love Yourself Journal, you will be able to see this section and then work out the details; if not you can open your own notebook and make an entirely new section. I would like you to record the definition you have of wisdom. Make it a strong paragraph. You can also talk about someone you believe is smart.

Everyone has their own answer to the question of what is wisdom and how it can be defined. Let me try to convey my idea of wisdom to ensure that you are aware of what I'm trying help you attain. I view wisdom as being something that is similar to the phrase "street intelligence." Street-smarts refers to having the ability to make best decisions in the right contexts. We often think of "book skills" in terms of the capability to work through math problems, and also to perform good work in the office or classroom. Street smarts is the ability to know when to request an increment, or to leave a room prior to an argument breaks out in the bar. It's all about the process of making decisions.

The ability to make wise choices when the opportunity is before you. That's my definition of wisdom, and that's the direction we'll strive towards. When you begin to appreciate yourself and become more charismatic as you grow, you will find yourself in the right place.

We're often unwise due to the fact that our subconscious and conscious desires aren't aligned. We tell ourselves that we want to earn more money however, we don't really do our best, we believe that wealthy people are dumb The first thing we'd ever take is an evening class. Your goals and actions aren't in sync. It's hard to gain wisdom when both parts within your head are at odds with each other.

Exercises

1. Every person has areas of wisdom in their lives - areas in which they are an expert and can make excellent decisions. Keep a journal in the Love Yourself Journal, write down an area where you believe you are a hefty amount of knowledge, a solid decision-making process, or significant amount of knowledge and you are comfortable in that knowledge. Note instances where others have acknowledged your wisdom , or sought your assistance, guidance or advice.

2. Write a lengthy essay about your inner knowledge - something you have a lot of knowledge about, but do not want to discuss. Perhaps you are able to comprehend the market for baseball cards or comics, or maybe you have a good idea about how boxers score matches. Note down a few words about an area of your expertise that you haven't spoken about with anyone else yet and the reason you've kept the subject secret from others.

Who do you Love?

You picked this book up in order to become someone that is loving themselves. However, love is slightly different for every person. We've all witnessed people in dangerous, abusive relationship or have a bad one, even though they claim they have a love for each other, and behave different. For certain people the definition of love is having someone they can do horrible things to and enjoy total control over. This is definitely not the definition I would use of love. We would like to be precise about what it is"to "love you."

I would like to give you the personal meaning of what is it to be a lover of yourself. I will also share what you are likely to accomplish when you go through this book, as well as the exercises and exercises.

1. Be confident in yourself completely.

A lot of people are perfectionists. we set ourselves to the highest standards and we expect levels of ourselves that we don't expect from anyone other person. When we do not meet our standards we are not able to forget about ourselves. We often find ourselves reliving the mistakes and foolish decisions that we committed in the past or in areas where we've failed ourselves. This impacts how we perceive ourselves.

If I asked you to assess yourself as a human on a scale from 1-10, you're likely to give yourself a score of three or five, or even seven. These are the most typical scores that people give themselves. If you don't see your self as a ten, nobody else will ever. Your world is limiting and that's an indication that you're not loving yourself enough.

2. Be aware that you aren't able to alter the past.

It's tempting to look back at the past and reflect on the choices you made and the things you would have liked to have taken a different course. It is possible to look back at instances when you did not take advantage of opportunities like friendship, jobs or even the guy or girl that you let go. I was in many friendships and relationships as a young person that have ended however I do not fret over the ones I had. Friendships were often lost before when social media was introduced. However, nowadays, people are within your life for the rest of their lives even if you don't wish to.

It is essential to recognize it is a fact that history has been written into stone, and can't be altered, so being concerned about it is futile.

We would like to put our time and effort into things that can change. That includes the present as well as the future. What you do "right right now" matters more than everything else. If you've committed errors in the past it's time to be honest with yourself and acknowledge, "I can't control or change the past. All I have control over and impact on are the current situation. That's where I'm going to be focused at the moment."

3. Accept yourself.

Everyone has flaws , and weak points. My imperfections aren't flawless, and I'm okay with that. I am who I am. Have ever been involved in a relationship who you thought wanted to change you they thought of you as an unfinished piece of clay that which they could mould into their own visions?

In my early 20s, I was with a woman who was determined to alter all of my characteristics. She wanted to alter my job and my college major and the music I was listening to, the clothing I wore, my city that I resided in, and my eating habits. When I asked her "Why are you trying to make me change so much?" She started crying and then said, "I don't want to alter you, what is it you're talking about?"

It's shocking that this relationship didn't work out. You shouldn't be in this kind of relationship with you either. If anyone can be able to accept you, it's your. Everyone has flaws and we all have weaknesses Just accept yourself and stop beating yourself up because you aren't "perfect."

4. Stay on your own side.

While in the highschool years I had a great acquaintance named Michael. I have vivid memories of how we got to know each other and I can even recall what he was wearing at the first time we got together. There was a girl who he was friends with who I really liked.

A couple of months later after Michael introduced us to one another, I ran into her at a restaurant and she saidto me "You don't be friends with Michael Do you?" She started badmouthing Michael, and I responded that to her "He is one of my friends and will always be. He is an excellent person." I didn't take advantage of an opportunity to make things happen for this girl, because I took a stand for my friend.

Then, shortly afterward, Michael was in a automobile accident, and later passed away. When she attended the funeral, I wasn't too thrilled however I was proud of myself since the only thing I did prior to his passing was protect my friend.

You ought to be like you are about yourself. Be yourself and stand up for yourself. Sometimes, people criticize you and make comments which can make you feel low. In these instances you may declare, "You just don't understand that I'm actually very proficient at this.. Even if you don't believe that something isn't a factor. I can say that the sky is brown, but it doesn't mean that I will be able to believe it. You are entitled to your own thoughts and views, and that's acceptable. You are free to have what you like however, I am a believer in myself. I am a part of my personal team."

5. Make sure you take your care of yourself.

Balance is the key to life. Thomas Jefferson believed that we ought to indulge in everything in moderation. It is important to be mindful of both the physical as well as the mental. You have to maintain your relationships with other people , and more importantly, your relationship with yourself.

The way we live our lives is classified in three areas: health, finances and relationships. If you're successful in two of these categories, and the third isn't and everything falls apart. You could have the most money on the planet but if you fall sick, then you've an issue which becomes the focus of your attention. The other strengths no longer have any significance.

Finding balance is crucial in all aspects. Try to find equilibrium both emotionally and spiritually by ensuring that your physical and mental health are in sync. Take charge of your body and demonstrate that you are tolerant of it. It is essential to take good care of your mind and show that you are concerned about it. This means that you should consume a healthier diet.

If you consume unhealthy foods it could affect confidence in yourself and stress levels. The thoughts we think about can also be triggered by brain's chemicals If we've got many bad chemicals in our bloodstreams that can trigger negative thoughts. There is a connection between the body as well as brain; care for both and both will get stronger.

6. Be proud of how incredible you are.

Nine people read this book but did not purchase it before you did and you decided to strengthen your relationship with yourself , which at least nine others didn't.

From the next 10 people who purchased the book, nine did not finish it; most readers don't even finish the books they purchase. We purchase books, only read the first part, and then we put them down particularly with non-fiction. I'm guilty of this as is everybody else. Since you've made it this long, you're beginning to distinguish yourself from the rest. You deserve to be proud of your achievements! You're proving that you're an exceptional person who is committed to making their lives better and should not forget this.

7. Be careful not to be too critical of your appearance.

This is a place that most people are involved. Sometimes, people make the effort to inform me that I'm ugly. I've received emails, and have also received comments from people in person. I've been told I am ugly in my appearance, I'm overweight, that I'm gross. But guess what? It doesn't matter; these people aren't important. All that matters is your opinion about yourself.

Some time ago at around thirty I joined eHarmony. I was intrigued by the website. It suggested to me only women who were at least 15 years older and fifty to one hundred pounds larger than my weight. This did not make me feel happy. It was discovered that eHarmony was a complete sham. My wife weighs half of my weight and just a little over half my age, and she believes I'm a very attractive man. This is all that matters You only have to find one person there who thinks you're pretty.

It's easy to be caught up in the things you think your flaws might be. The media interviews Victoria's Secret models all the often and ask "What is your least favorite body area?" And they'll say, "Oh, I hate my ankles. I don't like these sides of my butt. I am a bit irritated by this ear." Every person has something about them that's not ideal or that they're not content with. If that's all we think about the negative, then it's a waste of energy.

8. You can bring out the best of you.

It's not always necessary to be successful, but you need to be able to compete. I've made many errors in life, business and in relationships. I've invested in numerous projects that been unsuccessful. I've had to deal with situations that were too stress-inducing the idea was floated of suing one the other, but after we looked over the checklist of work I done, they stated: "Ok, you have done your best, but it's not your fault this project failed."

This is what people want an example of dedication and faith. If you're doing your best, you should not expect anything less. It's not always sufficient - you will not always be perfect in all things. However, as long as remain focused and strive to improve you'll keep growing as a person and feel proud about the work you put into.

9. Don't let other people drag you down.

The way you live your life plays out like a film and you're the protagonist. Everyone else are "extra" to the film of your life. they aren't even allowed to speak parts unless you let them to. In college I was in the love of a deaf woman and I had many deaf buddies. If any of them didn't like what someone said then they would just shut their eyes.

Close one's eyes represented the most blatant acknowledgment of the other person's presence It was a method to say, "I don't care what you say, I'm obstructing it." They could be able to easily remove someone's speaking part should they wish to.

We all have this power. What other people say isn't important unless you allow it. If someone has negative thoughts or attitude, you can do your best to ignore them. Remove them from your life, and forget about them They don't matter. They're not the main character of the show but you are.

10. Experiments are opportunities to learn.

No matter how good or bad and whether or not you make it or not each encounter is an opportunity to grow and develop as an individual. Even if the things you've experienced in your past weren't detrimental to your character, they only helped you grow. We learn more through our mistakes than our accomplishments, so any errors in the process are fine. If you think of your history as a string of events that led you to this moment then you should be thrilled about the fact that you are here. If your life had been slightly different, you may not be reading this book. I'm glad that your history has led you to where you are today.

Questions to Reflect

Take a look at your list of the ten items we've just discussed. Which of them are areas that you're already strong? What do you consider to be areas where you are weak? Do you have any areas where you are struggling? Are the words of others holding you back? Do you sometimes feel like you're holding yourself back due to mistakes you've done previously?

The more you learn about yourself and the more you go through these tests and tests, the faster you'll see the light at other end. Examining and identifying areas in which you have strengths and weaknesses will allow you to determine what you should be focusing on in your efforts in the coming weeks.

Introduction to Self-Esteem

Self-esteem is a different word that you hear used frequently. We frequently hear it mixed with self-confidence, however they're not the identical. Self-confidence refers to how strongly you trust in your capacity to achieve things. Self-esteem measures how you view your self-worth as an individual. Did you remember that I made you evaluate yourself using a scale from one to ten? That was a nifty self-esteem test.

Self-Esteem Engine

In case you did not catch it at the conclusion of the previous chapter, self-esteem refers to your mental and emotional belief in your worth and worth as an individual. It's how much you imagine you'd pay for yourself. It's more significant than how you feel inside. It influences your whole life. Your self-esteem can influence the way you make decisions as well as the goals you follow, and the possibilities you think of as possible. It's almost impossible to tell you how crucial self-esteem is. It is the foundation of of becoming awed by your own self, establishing a powerful image and creating the life you've always wanted to live.

If you're self-conscious If people present opportunities at your door and you are unable to accept them, you refuse them because you fear you'll be a failure. Someone comes up to you and tells you, "Hey, we would like to employ you for this project, and we're going to pay you twice the amount you earn in your present job." You decline the offer down because you believe that you'll try the task, fail, and then be unemployed, and then back to zero.

Case Studies

Let me offer you couple of examples to help you understand this one step more. Spend some time reading each of these cases and then reflect on the examples. Following each one of these cases There will be some reflection questions I'd ask you to complete within the Love Yourself Journal.

CASE 1. Mary is a highly intelligent girl and will begin her last year at high school in September. Despite her obvious intellectual capacity, Mary has very low self-esteem. She believes that she is an average student and, while her peers are aspiring to become lawyers or doctors She believes that she'll be lucky if she gets a job in a stable office. Due to the fact that her self-esteem has deteriorated and is impairing her thoughts, she's decided to study in the last year of high school which will hinder her ability to be accepted into top universities or colleges.

Question What will Mary's low self-esteem impact her life, both in the short - and longer-term?

CASE 2. James is a student at a college. He is driven to give back to his school and support his classmates, and he has a wealth of creative and innovative ideas. But, his self-esteem is low. has him believing that he doesn't have anything to contribute and that students on the council are smarter and more creative than he is. He is not running for the student council.

Question What do you think do you think James his low self-esteem impact his college experience? How will it impact his future life because of the choice he was forced to take?

Case 3 Meredith has a tremendous work ethic and is committed. In reality, she is probably the most efficient and committed employee at the office. But she is lacking self-esteem and continually underestimates her talents and what she contributes to the workplace. Because of this, she's not been able to get a promotion even though a lot of less able colleagues are screaming for one, and are content to get rid of the competitors.

What will be the impact of Meredith's low self-esteem impact her job prospects?

What is the current state Of Your Self-Esteem?

Then, take a look at yourself. What is the present state in your self-esteem? What do you consider to be your current level of self-esteem? What would you consider your self-esteem?

It's difficult to measure accurately our self-esteem since we're so comfortable with things being seen as we see them that we can't be objective any longer. It's going to take us a while to do some work to attain that. We tend to view aspects of ourselves as well as aspects that we consider ourselves to be normal and a natural element of who we are.

If you've had issues with self-esteem for many years it is possible that you're a realistic, not a pessimist "I do not have a low self-esteem. I've recently realized what I'm actually worth. I'm just self-assessing myself. My assumption that I will be unable to do this job is true." We are too ensconced in these belief systems that we begin to limit ourselves and are unaware of how badly our low self-esteem affects and harms us.

Self-esteem is a serious issue because it influences all important decisions we make in our lives and if it's low, it could turn into self-fulfilling prediction. We decline amazing opportunities because we aren't sure that we can succeed. We aren't confident in ourselves. When life doesn't go as we thought it would We forget all the opportunities we turned down and think, " I was always right. My life didn't go as smoothly in the way I thought it would. I was always right since the very beginning." We are able to feel that we've earned a righteous excuse, although it's not a valid reason to be unhappy.

Self-Esteem in 3D

Below are a few self-esteem-related questions to answer using either a "yes" or "no." We're going to utilize these questions to assess your self-esteem, and to create a 3-D representation.

As an ambulance driver volunteer I was taught how to connect lead leads onto the monitor for the heart. The basic configuration comprises four stickers. It is possible to put one on the ankle and wrist and can get a realistic two-dimensional view that shows the inside of the heart. For patients who are more serious or someone who is suffering from an attack on the heart or who is in a critical situation it is necessary to move into 3D and get the most accurate image we can get and, in this instance, we attached twelve leads. It is recommended to start with the basic four leads and then proceed to do an entire series of chest to view your heart at every perspective.

That's why we've got quite a few questions that we'd like to explore. Answer them all in a simple "yes" either "no."

1. Do you feel inferior to others?

2. Are you hard on yourself when making mistakes or fail to do something?

3. Do you find yourself constantly being a an observer rather than a an actual leader?

4. Do you have trouble to assert your opinions?

5. Do you experience a feeling of disdain toward you?

6. Do you often feel unsure about yourself?

7. Are you unsure if you are worthy of happiness?

8. Are the negative thoughts you feel about yourself make you more reluctant to

attempt new things and showcase your skills?

9. Do you often think that people don't appreciate you or are they judging you?

10. Do you feel scared to voice your opinion in front of other people?

Take your time putting together each of the above-mentioned questions and then award yourself a point for each answer. The more points or points you earn and the more work you must complete. When the "yes" answer is in the tens of a tenth or more, there's plenty of ground to conquer. If you only have just one or two answers you can count on us to have less many tasks to complete however we have to finish it.

Pause for time to think about your performance. Are you amazed by the way you responded to these questions? Are you shocked to discover that your self-esteem didn't quite match the level you imagined it should be?

If you're starting to panic, don't be concerned You are only beginning to recognize certain weaknesses in your self-esteem and it's much easier to address the issues. You're on your way towards success. If you continue studying this book, incredible things will occur. Make a note on the Love Yourself Journal how you are feeling about these results as well as any other things you observed while doing the exercise.

Questions to Reflect

In your Journal your responses to the following questions of reflection.

1. Are you shocked by the number of "yes" answer choices you provided during the test? If yes, what was the reason? What did you find surprising with your responses?

2. Consider each question and decide if you answered yes. What is the reason it was a "yes? What's holding you back in this regard? What's the cause of this particular self-esteem void?

3. Begin to think of ways to fix this harm. Are there trends that you've been aware of or have you observed things you've not thought of before?

Chapter 6: Unstoppable Confidence

Confidence is yet another word we often use without having a definition. We're used to hearing "He isn't confident enough. He's too confident. It is time to improve your confidence in yourself." In actuality the majority of us aren't sure what confidence means because the majority of people have their own definition of the word instead of the definition found within the dictionary. We have to come up with your own personal definition for confidence that we can all agree on, so that you understand what I'm saying when I talk about it.

I consider confidence to be the amount of faith you have in your capabilities. It's your own assessment of your capability to manage any situation. It is possible to feel confident in one field however not in another. You may feel confident in the boardroom however, the idea of talking to a beautiful male or female in a bar causes your knees shaking. It's terrifying.

For certain of us, our struggle with our overall level of confidence. We do not think that we are efficient as individuals. If you are lacking self-confidence, it can manifest itself in other aspects of our personalities. When we begin to display depression, and we are reluctant to accept chances, and then we turn down opportunities that come our way. Lack of confidence is usually the reason that we are unable to take advantage of the best chances in life, because we believe that we aren't equipped with the skills the skills required, and we aren't convinced that we'll be successful.

Questions to Reflect

Inside Your Love Yourself Journal, write down your answer to the following query: How confident are you?

It's always interesting for me to ask people about this issue. How they respond is as significant in the response itself. Certain people assign themselves scores on a scale from one to 10. Self-confidence levels for those with low self-esteem are three. People who have confidence in themselves have seven. It is not a popular choice to make a statement of ten, as it is pretentious, but having a self-confidence scale is actually the goal we're trying to achieve. That is what you ought to be aiming for.

What you believe in yourself, and how you express how you are convinced of your self is crucial. The way we express ourselves speaks how we think internally. thinking. Some people talk about confidence when compared to other people, "I am confident but I'm not as sure like Tim." Spend just a moment to write a few paragraphs, and then spend some time learning about yourself.

Parts of Self-Confidence

Self-confidence is a mix of other elements. It includes self-esteem. This is the amount you love yourself, or how much you believe that you are an excellent or worthy individual, but is also self-efficacy. As you might imagine, self-efficacy is an indicator of how efficient you think you are. One of the most famous examples that I am sure you will relate to is driving. The first time you step in the driver's seat of a vehicle there is no faith in your abilities to drive. There is no confidence in your abilities because you aren't sure what to do.

You may think and believe with confidence that you will learn to drive and have the capability to drive in your own self, but you do not believe that you can just take a seat in a car, press the button and start driving without anyone training you. If you're already able to drive, then you have an unshakeable confidence in your ability. You are confident that you are competent to drive since the experience has given you confidence and trust.

Before you move on into the next section Take a moment to think about these questions: do have confidence in your abilities? Do you think you are a good person? Do you think you're competent? Do you think you're an individual who is capable of accomplishing tasks? Are there any projects you could be putting before your right now that you are completely and completely incompetent to complete? If you had sufficient time believe you are capable of tackling any problem or challenge?

Confidence Test

Below is a test which can to determine what your confidence level is at the moment.

1. Are you willing to defend your opinions when it appears to be different from everyone else's?

A) Very or willing.

B) Not willing or unwilling.

2. How readily and easily do you admit mistakes that you've committed?

A) Very easily and without hassle or very quickly and easily. And then, I learn from them.

B) It is not easy or without extreme difficulty. I usually take great care to conceal my errors.

3. How much of your life is influenced by what others may think or consider?

A) A) Not much even or not at all.

B) A little or even a great deal.

4. Would you be willing to venture beyond your comfort zone to achieve something?

A) A) Yes, often or always will be.

B) It's not often or ever. I'm scared of failure.

5. How confident do you feel about your capabilities?

A) Positive or extremely positive.

B) not very either negative or positive.

6. How do you think about how you will respond to real-life problems?

A) Excited!

B) Afraid of. I'm scared of "showing myself to the world," so to speak.

SCORING: The more "A" responses you select more confident your levels are. If you picked a lot of "b" answers there is a lot of work to do in increasing your confidence in yourself.

Self-Observation Exercise

For a single day, you should keep the Love Yourself Journal handy, or, if it's too to be a hassle, keep your smartphone near, and every when you see you doing or saying something that shows low self-confidence, take an entry in your journal. If you're not certain which of these situations are happening then you can take a take a look at the test you took previously and then add the "b" answer as a low self-confidence response.

Look at your actions throughout the day. There are likely to be little "no-self-confidence" things that you're not even aware of which is exactly what we'd like to notice. We'd like to spend a day focusing on your identity and what you're accomplishing and how you are experiencing life. You might be noticing a gorgeous woman or man, but you don't speak to them. Perhaps you're sitting in the elevator alongside two other people at work , who are engaged in conversations that you would like to join in but don't. Perhaps someone is taking credit for your work and you don't speak up. You're in the gym and need to decide whether you want you want to take the beginner or advanced class. You opt for the beginner class, even though you are able to manage more advanced classes. When you experience something similar to this, you should take note of the event. We're trying to establish an outline of the current location of your life.

I am currently experiencing the same experience. The last week, I bought an exercise watch. It tracks every single thing I do. It records every step I make and every time I walk up a step and my heart rate is constantly monitored and everything else I do and it's always watching me. In the beginning I did not alter my behavior, but I just wanted to know my current state so that I could see the changes. I created an initial baseline before changing my behaviour.

I've been walking across my dock, writing this chapter for the entire day. At present, my watch tells me that I've been walking for three kilometers this morning. I've walked more than two thousand steps however I'm still required to take fifty-two hundred ninety-six feet in order to achieve my daily goals.

With my baseline information I can now assess how I am doing. I know how much exercise I need to do to stay at the same level and what I have to work on to get to an even higher level. We're trying to establish an understanding of your confidence in the same manner. With certain actions, I can improve the overall health that my body is in, you could do the same and utilize certain strategies to boost the mental health of your body.

After you have finished your day of tracking your self-confidence, add all the data you have collected into Your Love Yourself Journal and analyze what you felt like throughout the day. You can then answer the following questions.

Which areas of self-confidence issues have you noticed that you didn't know that you had a problem with? What did you think could be the reasons for these areas of self-confidence decline?

You might discover that each moment you experience low self-confidence moments the reason is that there's an attractive individual in the space or there is someone who is authoritative or perhaps it just occurs in social settings, not in business settings. This kind of data could aid you in focusing your efforts towards improving your self-confidence and perform better at the next time.

The Observation of others exercising

The rest this week be aware of the way people around you conduct themselves. Be on the lookout for indicators of self-confidence loss and other behavior that reveals their lack of confidence in themselves. We live our lives as narcissists and completely focused on ourselves that we are often unaware of the way others live and experience life. I'd like to alter your perspective. I would like you to observe how your surroundings alter. You can observe signs like people looking down instead of looking each other with eyes and people who are hesitant to give answers or sweating, every single one of these indications.

After a few days of observation it's time to the pages of Your Love Yourself Journal again and record what you've learned. If you discover that others are as anxious as you are it is a huge surprise. This is a huge revelation!

The Charisma Fuel

The most popular piece of advice given to couples is "There there is no thing more appealing than confidence. If you are looking to find the one you want to be with, you need the confidence to make it happen." We are aware that confidence is crucial. I was told this message often when I was younger and I often thought to my self, "Well, that is amazing, but how can I increase my confidence? Is there a trick to making me more confident? Do you have a specific method? Is there anything I could try?"

This chapter we're going to help bridge the gap between charisma and confidence. I'll discuss with you some strategies that I've developed through my sweat, blood tears and anger that I've shared only with my private clients I've worked with previously. However, I'm going to give them to you.

Experience is the best way to build confidence

If you follow this portion in the text, you'll develop into a highly confident person. I enjoy fighting mental challenges on the street. I prefer to combat them in areas where they're weak. The best way to build confidence is to be confident in yourself in real life. It's very simple.

There are many ways that you can boost your confidence, which we all know about: join the gym, learn new skills, and become stronger faster, more efficient, and smarter. These are all great and can assist a in a way however, we've all met individuals with fantastic bodies but have a lack of confidence. Confidence comes from being competent that is, being able to perform things and being able to do it effectively. Repeating something repeatedly will eventually bring you to the point that you're not worried about it.

One of my acquaintances was an army soldier. At one point I asked him about speaking to women. He was extremely nervous at the idea of speaking to an individual in a bar. I told him, "You just spent nine months in war. Are you anxious when you open an entrance and you realize there's something terrible in the other corner or the booby trap, or even someone shooting?" He said, "Talking to women makes me more anxious." I replied, "Well, objectively, talking to women is much safer than being in an area of war. Being a soldier can be an extremely dangerous profession."

At that point we realized that the reason for his insecurity wasn't objective. It was subjective. It wasn't an issue of reality, it was based on the perception of reality. We went a bit deeper and found that he'd practiced tens of thousands of practice sessions with his team doing door after door and had practiced in real life numerous times. He was aware that his team relied on him each when he completed it. Experience builds competence and confidence. Therefore, what we wish to accomplish is to show physical confidence.

Territory-Based Confidence

The best way to build confidence is to take control of territory. The greater the area you can control and the more secure you're. Take a look at the rich who have a large amount of land, they're more secure. We'll be doing the exact same thing however whether you own land or not is not important. I'd like you to start at your bathing area. I would like you to turn into an absolute monster, someone who obsessively examines every square inch in your bathroom. You will clean your bathroom, and then put everything back where it belongs. You'll be very strict as your bathroom is your home anyone who indicts your territory is declaring the war against you. This change in attitude will alter your life.

When you are the first to complain to someone about changing things in your bathroom, you may feel a little odd, but after the next and fourth time you begin to feel distinct; you'll begin to feel like an emperor. If you're sharing a room with a friend or share a bathroom, this is the way to say "This bathroom is my property which will remain what I would like for it. If you're planning to create an mess in the bathroom, you need to take me down first, as I own this area. I've claimed this area and you must respect the territory."

Expanding Territories

You are making a declaration of intention; you're placing your claim on the universe and change the way you look at the world surrounding you. It is an era of a place that is in a state of flux. We do not have a home of our own. The majority of us aren't working for a company that is in control. Our boss may dismiss us at any time or steal the cash away until the government shuts down the business. There are a myriad of ways to be fired tomorrow, and they are out of your reach.

It is a society in which only a few have control over our destiny or lives however, it's the time to get back your control. In my younger years, I wanted to wash the bathroom in spite of my wishes.

After I realized how effective this strategy could be I was my own bathroom cleaning. Each time I have an apartment mate, I bargain. I ask, "Are you willing to take care of the bathroom when I'm suffering from illness?" They go, "Oh disgusting, no!" Then I go, "All right; I will be the most thorough toilet cleaner but you'll have to wash your dishes, prepare, and do washing." They say, "Okay, fine." The reason I choose the bathroom was because it's small and takes a minimum of time to wash it. Even if your bathroom looks gross, at best you will spend an hour to get it clean and tidy.

After you have mastered the bathroom (this could take just a few days or weeks, which is perfectly okay) I'd like you to expand your boundaries; it's time to add your bedroom. As a child, I used to be extremely messy. When I was in the highschool years, I had never cleaned my space. I rely on my parents for it , and - surprise! I was at the point in my life that I was at my lowest. I'm now extremely strict about keeping my house.

Your bedroom should be flawless. It doesn't matter if you're single, married, or whether you share a room with a roommate or not, it doesn't is important. It's all about having control. Don't be a victim to on the other person. If they're a mess, this is an indication that they are powerless. Each time you tidy the mess of your roommate you don't have to be their servant. you're showing them that they're powerless and weak.

You tell yourself, "Your efforts to make your house tidy are going to fail each time. You may not want to clean off your clothing. You are free to leave your belongings all over. I will make sure to clean it and I will keep the room tidy because it is my home. It is my property and you don't have any influence over this space anymore. It is not your right the privilege of living in a mess of a home regardless of how much you'd like to." While they claim that they have transformed you into their home slave, they have actually given all their authority to them. They have renounced their confidence and self-belief.

If people come to your home and tell you, "Wow, the house is so tidy," your roommate very likely to say "thank you" and will accept the compliment. You should take one second. They have been stealing an compliment that was intended to you. Why? Because they are afraid to admit to reality. They don't want declare, "I do not clean the house. My roommate is, and I'm in power." The person who cleans is the one with the power.

There's a chance that you'll experience some moments of doubt in this moment in the beginning, wondering if I've fooled you. Stay focused. Within a couple of weeks, the dynamic in your home will change. If people enter the clean home only to notice that your roommate's space is filthy, they'll alter their perception. Cleaning is for an reason, so maintain that as your main goal in this activity.

Once you've taken control of your bedroom, you'll then be able to take over the living room and take over the hallway. Then, the entire house is yours to control. If your home looks stunning and you start to feel fantastic.

I am reminded of I remember a Latin quote that I learned in high school "A sound mind within a healthy body." It's very difficult for me to remain focused on my work when my home is messy and unorganized. If your home has been sloppy, it could distract you. If you're dating and you meet someone wonderful and they are tempted to go to your home and you think, "My house is messy," you won't bring them home as you're embarrassed and have missed out on a chance. It is possible that you have missed out on the person you love because you're not in control of your own life.

When you begin to take over more areas, your authority will be drastically altered. This isn't about fighting your roommate. This is merely an illustration of how strong you can be in relation to everyone other person living in your home. It doesn't matter if it's your spouse, children parents, your spouse, or your in-laws, it really does not matter.

Take Over the World

When you've got complete control of your home, it's time to take your car. In high school I attended school with very rich teenagers - we're talking about sixteen-year-olds with parents who purchased their Hummers as well as Ferraris. They had no respect for their vehicles; they were not interested in their cars.

I also attended school with a child who worked three years to buy a damaged car that was the most expensive that he could afford and the car was washed every day. He would walk up to the home, strip off his clothes and then wash his car just like in the 1980s in a heavy metal movie. It wasn't because his car was costly or because it was gorgeous and aesthetically pleasing, but because it was a reflection of his power over his own piece of the globe.

It is important to treat your car like you would treat your car. I don't care if your car is a bit of rubbish Stop saying it's this. I don't care whether your car costs one hundred thousands of dollars, or 50 dollars. It doesn't matter. It's yours and you are required to consider it to be part of your property.

As you control your car, you will learn how to fix your tire and replace the oil. eliminate those fast food wrappers, and then you begin to feel better. If people pass by your vehicle and ask, "Is this brand-new?" you'll feel great. They're not admiring your skills in cleaning; they compliment your dominance capabilities. They are recognizing your authority and authority.

The great thing about taking get control of your vehicle is that have now mobile control where the car travels the confidence of yours follows. You're beginning to show yourself that confidence is able to be carried with you wherever you go. It doesn't have to be that is tied to one place and we are able to move in it. Even if you begin with a low level this method will do wonders to boost your confidence. If you begin with greater confidence it might take several steps before you begin to feel the benefits. Once you've completed this workout you will have confidence that is an unshakeable ten and you'll be awe-inspiring.

Once you have mastered your car, it's time to begin using remote places. What is your cubicle like at work? It must be spotless. It must be spotless. It is not necessary to wait around for the janitor to take care of your desk. Are you five? Are you a teen? Are you my age at 16? No. You are able to and should be able to be in complete control of your world. Your workspace is an integral part of your universe.

If your boss visits your office and leaves the place messy, you tell him, "What do you think you're doing? You are my boss and I'll take on any task you assign me however, please do not create a mess in my work area. It is my space and I'm concerned for it." When your manager saysto you "I don't like your manner of conduct, and I am dismissed," you can take the matter to court and you'll win every time.

If your boss tells you, "I fired him because the office was not neat," he will lose the same amount ten times over and you'll make a living off the winnings. Nobody can dismiss you because you're an effective Steward. Nobody can claim, "He took too good care of his desk, the stewardship was too important to corporate property." When your manager complains to HR complaining about this and you're fired, it's likely to be next week, because every business needs to have a person to be a steward.

It's an extreme example however, this is the way your territory must be. It is not advisable to invade once you've staked your claim.

There's nothing better than those who are in control of their work space and feel trust in what they are doing. You can take over more and more areas of your workplace until you feel confident and comfortable before you also begin with remote sites.

I have extensive discussions in my books about networking about how you can take control of a place like an eatery or bar, and how you can become an individual who can dominate these social and public place. One of my friends used to wash glasses from his bar of choice. the barkeeper would scoop up the glassware from the messy tables, after the patrons had not put them in the bar. People would askhim "Do you work there?" And he would reply, "No, I just like to be somewhere nice."

I like it. He's bending the reality. He wasn't dressed as an employee, and the people were not convinced that they were bartenders; they believed he was the manager or owner. 18 years old, clearing glasses because he believed in his work and wanted the establishment to appear nice. And people believed he was superior to the bartender he actually was. He was exuding an amazing degree of confidence.

The more you conquer in addition to the longer you concentrate on it in the context of assuming territories, the greater your confidence will grow. What's cool about this method is that you don't even need the thought of confidence. it's just a side result. You'll be so focused on getting into the game and impressing people that the effect will be an enormous increase in confidence.

The Facets of Charisma

There are many other aspects of charisma. Take a look at how each one of them can be applied to your life and the amount or lack of it you have of each.

1. Energy. As human beings, our levels of energy can increase or decrease dependent on the environment who are around us. We all know the expression, "Misery loves

company." If someone is weak in energy and comes into the room then the entire room's energy levels decrease.

Humans are emotional creatures. Our emotions can be compared. When you're in a space with someone who is very active you will feel all the enthusiasm. Consider the person whom you refer to as "the person who makes your party." This is the kind of person you'd like to invite at every gathering to ensure all guests are having a great time. They're energetic and they bring everyone's enthusiasm upwards, they lift people's joy up. This is the primary characteristic of charisma.

2. Positive thinking - believing that positive things are possible and seeing the best in others as well as seeing the best of the entire world and recognizing that things are improving. There are people I know who discuss how everything will go to the brink of hell. They are always discussing politics and the state. They constantly talk about the fact that the currency is about to fall and the world is heading into war and that the Illuminati will take over the world and

kill all of humanity. I am not a fan of them. They take my joy away and who would want to be around them?

People who are optimistic, even people who seem overly optimistic are wonderful to surround yourself with. You think, "Wow, this person is so content; ignorance truly is bliss." I'd prefer to not be informed about what's in the news as there's no good news there. People who are optimistic are very attractive.

3. The excitement to try new things. Here's an example. You are required to take an excursion for work and you must take one person who is either Tom or Susie. You tell Tom, "Hey Tom, we will be taking an excursion for business this weekend" Tom says, "Ah man, are you telling me something? I don't want to be working on weekends. Are you planning to compensate me for overtime? What if I've got plans?"

Then , you say the exact similar thing to Susie and she says, "Oh my gosh, Please bring me! I'm so thrilled! I am a huge fan of traveling, and I've got the best new CD of travel mixes. I am eager to go out and about along with you." Part of you may think that you shouldn't listen to Susie's CD of road mixes and I totally understand this, but at the very the very least, she's enthusiastic.

You'd rather be around someone who is excited about the trip and is positive about the experience. The word "enthusiasm" is a mix of enthusiasm and energy.

4. Engagement. Certain people are extremely reserved They are not inclined to talkand tend to keep their thoughts to themselves. This is not charisma. Charisma is about putting your energy out into the world. The only way to pour that energy out into the universe is to engage and interact with people around you.

I'm naturally shy This is why I don't like talking with other people living on the same island. You wouldn't know it however, since the only time you'd see me will be at a convention. When I'm out networking for my business I am able to activate the social aspect that makes me a person.

I talk for three months to no one, then in just three days I'm talking to everybody at all times. I shut off my energy levels until I am in need of them. It's the same similar thing.

5. Intelligence. It's not only about being smart. It is about showing your ability to think. There are many kinds of intelligence. There are people I know who do not have the ability to read, however when they are in the wilderness they are able to be able to survive in any situation. The notion of IQ is the only and all of intelligence is a nonsense. It doesn't matter the area you are smartest in and it's all about demonstrating that it.

If you're extremely adept at knots, be sure to inform people. It's fun. People are drawn to knowledge and interests. If you can show them something you're good at and know the basics of you, they will be drawn into it.

I know a person who can build a complete home by himself. Anyone who meets him might think that he's stupid since he's not a book-smart person or even smart at all. In the majority of aspects of intelligence, he's not extremely strong however, when he steps in the house and starts picking up an instrument, he's incredible. When he's working on a project and working in a continuous manner and is extremely charismatic. I love watching him build. I tried to assist him once however I'm so bad using tools that I amn't allowed to do it anymore.

6. Make it an interesting. What is the challenge? It's like going towards the comedian and telling them, "Hey, be funny."

Here's how to make yourself more intriguing: do what you like. Do not do what others would like you to do and begin doing whatever you like to accomplish. If you're a senior and would like to become proficient at ice skating, try it. It's a lot more exciting than watching TV.

As a teenager still in school was convinced I had to go through every television show to be able to discuss what was on. I was looking to be part of what I would call "culture." It was my dream to wanted to be a part of the conversation whenever someone was discussing a show. For a while I was able to accomplish this, but I had no real relationships. I didn't have real friends, and I had no conversations. I was boring.

If you are able to establish extraordinary hobbies, those that are distinct from the usual activities, then you start to become fascinating. However trying to be popular and trying to be like everybody else is the most serious error you could make since it will make your life boring. You turn into a flat character and become a stereotype.

A lot of people want to challenge mainstream culture , and to say that "I differ from everybody and everyone else!" And they are in a crowd of twenty others wearing the same clothing and playing the same songs as well as doing similar thing. To be unique you must do something interesting, and there is always something unique in your that you'd like to pursue. Perhaps you haven't done it because you believed, "It is too simple and boring and it's not very popular." Do it nonetheless, no matter what it is, since doing what you love will make you more attractive.

7. Be assertive. When you are around other people, they're going to try to push back at your confidence to determine how strong your self-confidence is. When I was single

Girls would always ask questions to try to make me doubt my self. This was not because they were evil however, they were trying to determine whether I was confident in myself. There are many people who create a false sense of self-confidence that does not exist. Sometimes , people will tell you things which are rude or hard to determine when you try to counter. They are looking to determine whether you have backbone. And it's much better to be on your feet, rather than sit on your knees. Nobody will ever be a follower of someone who is not assertive and that is a fact.

8. Excellent interpersonal abilities. The most charismatic people are great in interacting with others. I discuss advanced interpersonal abilities in this book as well as in other books of this series as it's an essential element. It is possible to become proficient in interacting with people. One of the most effective methods to achieve this is to ask questions of their lives and being genuinely interested that leads to the ninth suggestion.

9. Be interested in others. People used to say that Bill Clinton made you feel as if you were the only one in the room. He created the feeling of the most important member of the group and he was the President. When there is a President in a room with another person it is the case that the other person isn't a factor. It is only the President who is the most important. However, he was able to achieve this by making people feel special. He had his amazing abilities and made him go towards his place in the White House two times in two years.

The art of faking interest with other people is a difficult task. It is much more effective to learn the art of convincing others. Find a way to become attracted to the lives of others. Each whenever I meet someone new I inquire about they do for a living. I would like to meet one person from each job. This allows me become more attracted to other people and makes me more attractive.

10. True leadership. It isn't easy to be a leader. People often think of leadership as telling people the right way to go. True leadership comes when your team is

suffering. A true leader would send his soldiers to death and then suffer from nightmares throughout his life. That's what leadership is. True leaders will work overtime and invest additional hours so that his team doesn't need to be reduced. He would fight for his team, that's leadership. It is not about being seated on a throne. it's all about how much weight you put that is on your head. The head is heavy because it has the crown. When you lead by sacrifice rather than greed, you're a true leader. People will want to follow in your footsteps.

Reflection Questions

Write these answers within the Love Yourself Journal.

1. Have you ever been called charismatic or claimed that you're an excellent leader? What did you think? What was you doing during that moment? What part of your personality did they respond to?

2. How charismatic do you appear on a scale from one to 10? In the case of a character from a video game What number of points would you assign yourself to show your

charisma? What are some ways you can do now to increase your charisma?

3. Think of your most charismatic persona. It is a person you've met in real life that is extremely charming. Give them a detailed description. My most memorable avatar was a man named Nathan. I had the pleasure of meeting him during high school and was fascinated by his way of treating people. He taught me to become well-known. I modeled myself after him and eventually became similar to him since the man was good and helped me become a better person.

4. Consider a few charismatic individuals that you admire, whether they're individuals you know on the street, seen on TV or even you've read in books. Consider what characteristics they share. Are there any traits on the list you share with them? Do you know of any other aspects that I haven't covered before?

5. What do you think an increase in charisma will impact your life? Do you think it would improve your relationship life, your work life, or your relationships? Will it

increase your happiness? What will your life look like different after you have come out your other half and are more attractive?

A Triad for Success

Many people consider charisma to be an intangible force or a mysterious quality individuals possess or lack since birth. It's something we cannot observe directly, we only have the ability to measure its results. It is difficult to determine if someone is charismatic in a solitary. If you have a charismatic individual and put them in a closed room, and it's impossible to determine their charisma. It's only apparent when other people are in the room to see how this person's charisma affects them.

If we are struggling with the concept of popularity and charisma and charisma, we see it as the missing ingredient that we either possess or don't have. There is no way to change it, since it's hard to gauge it within us. It is difficult to gauge my charisma by talking to anybody else, or without engaging with other people and watching the way they react. It's hard to determine what we can do to improve our performance.

Self-esteem and confidence are essential aspects of charismatic individuals. People who radiate confidence positive energy, confidence and faith in themselves attract people towards them. The more faith you have about yourself the more people trust yourself. Consider the great leaders of the past and even leaders who were misguided. They had a strong influence since they believed that in them so deeply so that, even when they made mistakes the people listened to them. This is the force of their charisma as well as their self-confidence.

Before you can gain confidence in your abilities to achieve your goals you must increase your confidence in yourself, self-esteem and how much you feel you're a good person. It's hard to strive for excellence when you don't love yourself or do not believe in yourself and you don't believe you're enough.

Things to Consider

1. Consider the most captivating people you have met; it could be people from your life or who are on TV. It is possible to look up historical leaders who have been influential throughout history. I had a friend in college who would listen to amazing speeches from the past. He thought that if was listened to enough speeches of charismatic leaders that it would make him into a charismatic. This didn't work.

Have a look at the most famous people you know and from the past, and then evaluate their credibility. Do you see something that is common? If you examine specific examples, you'll be able to recognize that there is a significant correlation between charisma and confidence individuals. It is not always easy to become charismatic however, every charismatic individual definitely has a lot of confidence in their appearance to the world.

Are you starting to recognize the connection between charisma and confidence? If you believe that I'm off, that's okay put it inside Your Love Yourself Journal. It's okay for you to not agree, and to to push yourself to start to think about these thoughts. It's all about helping your thinking process grow.

2. It is a good idea to think about the motives behind the connection between charisma and confidence. What is it that you believe confidence makes us appear more appealing to others? If you think of someone in real lives who has charisma, do think that their confidence was the reason you were drawn into their circle?

3. After you've been through this journey for just some time are you feeling more at ease and confident about this journey? Do you have specific steps you plan to take to further progress through this path to be more attractive? Maybe you've already completed certain steps.

4. Consider a moment you encountered someone with a low self-confidence. Or perhaps an instance where someone displayed an utter lack of confidence in themselves. Did you observe a similar low self-esteem? When you first noticed it did you feel repelled or depressed by the force of their self-confidence issues? Now having a better understanding, can you see the

reason we avoid those who lack confidence in themselves? Do you have a different view of the present situation as you did in the past?

Reviewing the Past Exercise

We will now look at eight scenarios and I'd like you to think about each one. Consider a time in which you were in each scenario, and then write your thoughts within Your Love Yourself Journal.

1. Consider a time when your insecurity prevented your ability to convince others to do something. Perhaps you were trying to convince a friend to watch a particular movie , but weren't confident that the movie was worth it or you made the right choice. So, instead of leading someone to a place they may not enjoy You let someone else choose and then went to see a movie that you did not like. Whatever the case you're trying to record it inside the journal you keep in your Love Yourself Journal.

2. Consider a time in your life that your insecurity hindered you from speaking out even when you could have had the courage

to speak up or had the courage to take actions. Perhaps you remember one of those tales from high school that every student has, in which the people were making fun of some one, and you wished you'd done something to stop them from doing so.

3. Imagine a time in your life that your self-confidence issues prevented you from pursuing a ambition. Do you have a desire to take on sports into the college level? Have you ever considered an artistic career but thought you weren't good enough? Perhaps you didn't believe that you were able to reach the next level.

4. Did your insecurity hinder your studies? I had a buddy who was far superior to me. He was an autodidact self-taught and played five instruments and was even offered a award to go to college, but he chose not to take it because he believed that he was stupid. He believed that he didn't have the skills and decided to put off his studies. Have you had an experience similar to this in your personal life?

5. Have you ever had a moment when your insecurity interfered in your career? Perhaps you didn't submit an application for the job you could have had or didn't ask your boss for a promotion or tell him, "You don't need to employ someone else, I'm capable of doing it."

6. Do you remember the times you were frustrated? An instance when your personality was sucked up within you and you were unable to communicate the way you would like to. It was difficult to find your words and feelings You felt stuck in your head and couldn't speak to the world the way you would like to. Your charisma could not be escaped.

7. What was the time that others' perception of your lack of charisma stifled you back? Perhaps you were on a team of speakers working on a group project and you were like, "Hey, let me be the speaker!" They said, "No you're just helping make the slides. You aren't a professional at being an effective speaker."

The last time I was elected to office while at high school. There were eight seats in the

Student Senate for my class and I came up with an amazing proposal - the entire strategy to make the school more effective. I came up with my idea of a donation program to provide clothing and school supplies for children with less privilege. The school I attended was prosperous school and I observed all these people dumping their clothes. I asked, "What if we did something better?"

After I had my talk just like everyone else, the students decided to vote against me. They told me, "You have great ideas but you're not attractive enough." They chose the most popular students and there was no change. Actually, a lot of the winners from the contest for popularity came to me and wanted to know my strategies so that they could try the ideas I had suggested, however didn't because the they didn't have enough ideas.

Implementation is the key to success. However, I learned a lesson the next day that believing in something wasn't enough. If I was unable to draw people to my charm and enthusiasm, then my concept was doomed to die. Did this ever happen to you?

8. Do you ever feel stuck in a loop, going from low self-esteem to low charisma and then low self-confidence then back again? People aren't interested in the things you say. They speak negatively about you, and declare that you're not a leader. They may say that you're not sure how to handle yourself, which makes you feel embarrassed and then stop believing it.

It is possible that you were not always within this cycle. However, maybe there was a point that you felt stuck in the cycle. Consider how you felt at the moment, and then consider how you feel when you look back at the time.

Conviction as well as Charisma Experiment Exercise

Another charisma and confidence method that I haven't yet divulged to you until now. This technique is extremely effective It has been used by me before, and it has been an empowering experience for me. It works well as a combination with the confidence-based on territory method. You may have heard of this before. It is known as "fake the illusion until you master it." Knowing the mechanism behind this technique is crucial to its effectiveness.

In your Journal In your Journal, make a the version 2.0 that you are. If you've been through one of my previous books and you've completed the procedure before, it could be the right time to make an 3.0 version. Create a picture of yourself who is incredibly charismatic and has extremely impressive levels of proficiency and self-esteem. Define the person you'd like to be. Imagine you're six months away from the present and write your thoughts in full detail. Create a 3D model of yourself in your head and record every detail within Your Love Yourself Journal. The edition 2.0 is the best in charm and confidence. It's the person you'd wish you were.

Once you've developed this character and you have the confidence to know how confidence appears when applied to yourself, you'll have to devote the rest of the week playing the role of this character.

You'll play acting for seven days playing the role of 2.0 and 3.0. You're playing a character that requires you to ask yourself "What 2.0 would 2.0 be like or say?"

Take a week to observe the way this character behaves. It is possible to go through one phase in which you're to far and in the opposite direction. I've experienced this myself. I modeled a certain self-confident me but it was too far and then became a jerk which is why I calibrated my self over the next week. That's okay. It's better to push it too far and then ease it back instead of spending the remainder day wondering if it was enough confidence.

Make up a persona for one week. Each time someone asks you an inquiry, you tell them what you 2.0 could be saying. After every day, when you return home, go to the Love Yourself Journal and respond to the following questions:

1. Did you receive different treatment from people in a way that made you appear more appealing? How did you feel when you were acting like a completely different person throughout the day?

2. What do you think that your self-confidence change has influenced your personality? Did acting more confident increase your charisma? Do fake confidences create charisma?

3. After you've completed this exercise and pretend that you are more assertive, do truly feel more secure? Do you feel that you have achieved permanent improvements in your confidence and level of charisma?

4. Do you feel this exercise has increased your self-esteem?

5. Do you plan to continue this workout for the rest of your life? Do you think this exercise will become an integral element of your daily routine?

If you are able to spend enough time trying to appear like a better self, then you'll turn into the same person. This is an extremely effective method. It begins on the other side in the range. The process begins in your interactions with other people. It begins with the outermost part that is your character.

If you combine them with our confidence-based on territory technique, which begins from your center it is two times as fast. The two techniques work effectively when used in conjunction. They are incredibly powerful.

6. Do you intend to stay to this method and continue using it? Do you enjoy watching the results work? Do you want to be that person every day, without being consciously doing it?

7. If someone came up to you today and said to you, "You read that amazing book. How can I make myself more attractive?" What would you advise them on? What steps can you recommend to someone else looking to be more charismatic?

Chapter 7: What Is It Mean To Love Yourself

Say you love yourself to someone and you'll get three different opinions. One of them would probable be arrogant. Another would be that you're an individualist as well as an arrogant narcissist. The third one, which will more often be received from the people who truly know you best is that you're wonderful.

CONCEIT

Conceit, as it is defined, is an over-inflated confidence in oneself or of self worth. Self-esteem or being aware of and valuing one's talents as well as achievements is a great thing. When everything goes to your head and you start to being arrogant and proud and then you become conceited.

Here's a short test to determine if you are really loving or are just being a bit cocky about yourself:

1. Your accomplishments and achievements prove how remarkable you truly are.

2. You don't like the company of those whose accomplishments and achievements are not as impressive as yours.

3. You dismiss the accomplishments and achievements of others, and you are frightened when they seem to be more successful than your own.

4. It is your responsibility to blame anyone who is responsible for failures or failures.

5. Respect and respect.

If you're having trouble disputing every point of the test, and then excuses or denial that none related to you, then you might face a few challenges to face. This is putting it mildly.

EGOTISM AND NARCISSISM

The world is not a fan of egotists or self-centered narcissists. They absolutely hate those who believes the sun shines through his back or that the universe revolves around his little finger. The world reserves viral content and sleazy gossip columns only for those who's favorite pronouns are me, I and me. However it displays its disdain for those who are obsessed with themselves that they believe they're the definition of perfect. Hollywood, Bollywood and the paparazzi might throw up an obelisk, a runway or stage for these however, in the end people are shocked that they don't have any other attention or interest other than praise and pedestals to stand on.

Narcissism, egotism and conceit all share a common factor that isn't love the vanity. Is loving yourself simply a display of self-importance or something more? Let's take a look at a case of selflessness and determine whether it resembles an authentic love for yourself:

MARTYRDOM

The world is full of martyrs. It lauds those who to give up everything, including their own identity to serve other people. It lauds those who willfully give up even their lives to serve the greater good. It is a tribute to the likes of Mandela, Gandhi and Pope Francis 1. For many it is the best instance of selfless love.

What is it?

A few psychologists believe that martyrdom, although appearing to be a noble cause but is actually a manifestation of megalomania. They also believe that many self-proclaimed martyrs are actually egotistical and arrogant beings. In the midst of selflessness and professed charity for others, lies the dark motive motivated by the desire to be an "living" saint. Or contemporary hero. The study of some famous last words, such as the ones who were about to die in the name of a cause, have revealed the motivation behind their place in the history of mankind to be protected or acknowledged with a revered spot near the throne God.

Simply stated, martyrdom is another form of humble brag: Justin Bieber going around town performing acts appropriate to Mother Teresa and bragging about it on Twitter.

St Paul offers the best insight into what is meant by loving yourself.

You're Really Loving Yourself

The text draws a line between true affection and hollowness that is exhibited by the three that were described by him in terms of "sounding brass or vibrating cymbals." These characteristics of true self-love can be described like this:

KIND, LONG-SUFFERING, AND LONG

It's simple to be intolerant or suffer for long periods of time with the rage of children and the whining of friends, or the inappropriate behaviour of bosses, strangers and coworkers. It's not too difficult to show kindness to strangers. But when it comes to you You are either angry or dissatisfied with your efforts. You could also be aggressive and demanding, often requiring to be too much or setting yourself up to an expectation that is higher than what you set for other people. It's not self-respect and could be motivating.

Being truly loved by yourself is offering yourself the same freedom to learn and grow from the mistakes you have made that have impacted others. Also, it means taking care of yourself first and recognizing your weaknesses and not being too harsh on yourself. It's not about constantly asking "what's to be gained from this" instead of giving yourself praise for a job well-done by allowing yourself time to develop and grow, and accepting that you won't be Superman all the time.

Not PUFFED UP, AND DOES NOT PARADE SELF

For those who believe that loving yourself implies being egocentric, St Paul has these to say: don't get overly exaggerated and don't show off.

To comprehend how being over-inflated and flaunting your love is just examine Hollywood, TMZ and the tabloids to see what these stars are doing to get the attention and spotlight. It's more annoying to see this kind of self-aggrandizement and false sense of entitlement among others.

Love yourself doesn't mean that you shouldn't be focusing on your wants, needs and goals, or acknowledge and recognize your talents abilities, talents and skills. Showing off your talents in front of others and having people acknowledge your beauty is in fact an expression of insecurity, rather than loving, and it's not always in need of an arena or runway to show off and be paraded on. There is no need any of that if you are truly loving yourself.

Thinks there is no crime

One of the greatest qualities of truly loving yourself is to not be negative about the person you are. This doesn't mean denying of imperfections, flaws or inadequacy. Instead, thinking nothing is not degrading yourself until you have lost your self-esteem and self-esteem.

When you consider yourself as being too stupid or incompetent to make a change for the better, then you are being negative about yourself. This is also true as when you think it's your destiny and fate to find yourself in a mess because you've been there for many years. Being a liar and not loving yourself can lead to finding an issue with every incident in your life , even been if your universe was conspiring against you.

REJOICES IN THE TRUE

Joy in the truth means acknowledging the things you already are and what you have the potential to be. Recognizing strengths, weaknesses and positive qualities as well as potential areas for improvement is the hallmark of truly being loved by yourself. Resentment for anything other than adulation refusal to acknowledge any error or wrong, and the anger at any assertion of infallibility an indication of narcissism vanity and conceit but not true affection for oneself.

Believes, hopes and perseveres

Any person who is able to remain hopeful and trust in his own abilities despite challenges and difficulties and who willingly takes on and endures the worst of things is truly a person who loves herself or himself. Someone who surrenders in frustration and is unable to find hope is one who is ready to give up being a person who loves himself. One who has lost self-esteem as well as personal dignity and has lost faith in himself is not able to declare that they love himself.

There's more to the epistle of the apostles that explains the meaning of loving yourself, but these ought to be enough to tell you if you're just drowning in self-pity or really must learn to take care of yourself. If the latter, go on reading.

Be aware of who you are

To be able to enjoy yourself and be content there are three key actions to follow. These are:

1. Be aware of who you are

2. Accept who you are.

3. Learn what you can be.

Let's talk about how to begin:

Find out Who You Really Are

What is it to identify yourself?

Knowing who you are is more than having your personal name and biographical data and your parents' lineage or your genetic background. Being aware of who you are is discovering your identity and what you are here for. Many a socialite has stunned the world with their miserable despite their lavish lifestyle and the possession of every desirable item or gadget. They drown in drugs, alcohol or sexual activity to find a purpose to their lives. Some turn to ascetism or even extreme religious practices to achieve this meaning. There are those who have no peace except for the effects of an addiction, cut wrist or a shot to the forehead.

Three things to assist you in discovering who you really are and start loving yourself.

You are unique

This is true. In the seven billion people around the globe currently, there isn't anyone as like you. Perhaps there are people who have the same color of skin and genes, or even behavior, but there isn't anyone who is a perfect copy of you.

What is that?

Simply put, you have potential, talents as well as dreams, obstacles and a few gems of wisdom nobody else has, and that's not even within your own family. Being without legs, skills or opportunities doesn't diminish your uniqueness , it only enhances it.

In the end, since you are an individual You are the unique element without which the human picture will never be complete.

You're a creditable customer

It may be difficult to believe, but until you get to the point of no return called life, you'll never be able to tell. The value you have is not measured by the amount of money you keep in your pocket or in the bank. It's not determined by the size of your assets or the power you hold. It might not even be within the realm of influence you enjoy over others who are around you.

Your value is comparable to the value of a diamond that is encased in rock. Even though miners haven't dug out the mine shaft or released it from its rock prison doesn't mean that diamonds aren't important. The fact that you're not isolated and possibly insignificant before the eyes of others is not a sign that you are without value and unimportant. Be aware that even a single one iota might be small, however, its absence does not mean that you are insignificant.

You aren't what OTHERS think you are.

Psychologists have noticed of children who are not given any positive reinforcement, and who are continually told that they are not good enough after each error. While a lot of children were raised with this mentality but there were some who have resisted the naivety and did not follow the same path like the rest of us. Man is influenced by the environment around him and be in the influence of the people around him, but a part of his individuality lets him break away from the shackles of conformity when given the opportunity.

As beautifully illustrated in the iconic film Gattaca There is no gene that can create humans to be human. There always will be a person who is willing to go against the grain and will break away from the group and create his own path.

This is simply a way of saying that despite the long line of generations before you, you're not who others think you are. There isn't a fate or destiny other than the one you decide to do with your life. Others can bind your hands, label your name, or force you to follow their wishes and transform you into their image However, only if consent to them doing so.

Your are Child of the Universe

There are people who find the comfort of claiming to be people belonging to the race of the master. Others believe that they are descendants of a long line of human evolution over millennia. Others consider themselves God's children. God.

Whatever the case whatever it is, one thing is to be certain about. In a million, billion trillion possible possibilities, and possibilities there is only one similar to you. And you are one of 7 billion people in a universe that is just one of the billion possible worlds in one million galaxies within the universe that is infinitely expanding. Some may consider this irrelevant, but the reality is that there's only you: the one element is the only reason why the universe could never be perfect.

Accept the person you are.

Acceptance is an enigma with two sides.

On the one hand, you can accept that your current circumstance is because of fate and be content with the rules it imposes. However, the other option is to acknowledge your uniqueness and worth and let go of the rest.

In the process of you are learning to love yourself accepting fate or karma is to do against yourself and deprive your self of the possibility of a better future. It's not really loving yourself to declare, "I accept my fate. I am submitting to the karma of my life." When you do this, you give in to pride in martyrdom as well as the pride-driven stubbornness which is only present in a narcissist or self-centered person.

Here are the things that you must accept, without resigning:

Recognize your weaknesses

There is no perfect man, but many people deny their shortcomings and are unwilling to admit their mistakes and failings. It's not love yourself, if you do.

You have to learn to recognize the fact that things are beyond your control that limit your possibilities or abilities. This does not mean that you should give up your independence to the forces of nature, but as a master tactician, you must be aware of what you can do to improve, strengthen or build upon. For example, an alcoholic who realizes that his love to be with his bar-goers is what fuels the addiction, realizes that he must quit the bar for the sake of being treated. However an alcoholic who claims that he wants the comforts of the bar as well as his acquaintances, will not achieve his goal of overcoming his addiction for alcohol.

A big part of knowing who you are is recognizing your shortcomings, your mistakes and the limitations you have.

Recognize Your Strengths

As everyone has weaknesses, everyone have strengths. This is the reason you are unique. It is possible that society has discovered this and is now trying to eliminate it by making you believe that you aren't. One of the most important aspects of knowing who you are is being aware of your strengths. A big part of being happy is acknowledging your qualities and making those part of you, regardless of what society tells you. Consider Beethoven who was a musician deaf who composed a number of the most famous masterpieces in the world. Or Handel who was starving and poor when he composed his famous oratorio The Messiah. J. K. Rawlings was a poor woman on a train at the time she came up with the idea that was a seven volume bestseller, and a string of box office successes. Alexander Graham Bell may not be acknowledged in the field of speech pathology, where Bell first began but the world is aware of Bell as the creator of telephones.

Your strengths might not match the way society views or values them but they are still strengths and you must increase them in order to become a better person.

Be proud of who you are

The world of today is filled with imitations and idol worshippers.

Everyone is aspiring to be the next Beyonce or the next Obama or the next Oprah. There is a lack of desire to be who they are like Bon Jovi did in his song. If that's not enough then there are people who don't even want to be anyone and instead appear to be a lost person in the crowd or a cog in the hordes of humanity.

It's not right.

If you want seeking to be a better person, you have to learn to appreciate the person you are in your own uniqueness, as well as your uniqueness. You need to learn to appreciate the person you are regardless of how society treats you and beats you down.

Take Choice, and be Accountable

The last step is accepting the obligation of making a choice and the responsibility that comes with the decision. This is the most challenging especially for someone who has experienced nothing but depravity, rejection or disappointment since the beginning of time. It can be a challenge to acknowledge shortcomings, as one realizes the consequences of the decisions made. But these are the most significant evidences of truly loving yourself. You can't claim to be in love with yourself, after having identified and accepting who you truly are but if you're unwilling to make the decision to let go or accept responsibility for your decision. Making the choice to leave your fate or karma amounts to renunciating your love for yourself , and the dignity that comes with it respect, self-esteem, self confidence and self-worth. This is the case when you attempt to avoid or deflect your own responsibility for the results of your choices in the past. However the decision to be yourself as you really are and accept responsibility for what you choose to do, will increase your determination, confidence and faith. It will enable you to not speak evil about yourself, to revel in your uniqueness and to believe in yourself in yourself, and then bear and endure the long-term suffering. You might not be able break free from the rigors of life, but you will have learned to appreciate yourself and attain a degree of satisfaction.

Have you made that decision?

Do What You Want to Be

You've successfully completed those two first steps of becoming a better person. You've discovered who you really are. You've accepted your flaws strengths, strengths and values. You've made a decision to be who you are.

Here are some steps you can take to become who you are:

Set a Goal

Setting goals is similar to making a map to get to your destination. It's an important thing to be aware that you must get into New York. It is an additional thing to plan your journey towards New York. Sitting in your home and fantasizing about getting there New York and what you will do when you arrive there will not bring you closer to the target. It is important to determine how much your trip will cost, the amount you'll need to put aside and what you have to do in preparation and begin to work on the plan. Keep in mind that a trip isn't just one huge leap, but it is a series of steps you must complete one at a time. It is possible to try out the art of making huge leaps but unless you are certain that the universe gives you immense power, you may decide to take these steps.

Believe that you can achieve

The next step after you've set a goal to be the best you can be is to trust. It will also bring out the flames of being yourself and igniting these flames into a fire that gives you confidence and confidence in yourself.

Being confident that you will succeed isn't a problem if you break your goal down into something achievable and when you persevere with faith and perseverance.

Step by Steps

This is the same as setting the goal and believing that you'll be able to achieve it. The art of making massive leaps isn't impossible but you don't have someone who can show you how to do it , and doing it yourself can take a long time. But, do you remember when you were a little one trying to walk? Apply that concept then apply that principle to your goals by breaking it into manageable steps, or goals that can be measured and that will help you build your confidence.

If we go back to the example of traveling for a trip to New York, your baby steps will likely be to save on a trip to the airport. this could even be broken down into just a few dollars per day until you've enough to purchase a ticket to The Big Apple.

Keep going

A child who takes few steps and then goes back to crawling won't be able to walk unless it is standing up and taking some more steps. Also, you'll never reach your goal if you abruptly give up after a few stumbles. Keep in mind that there's never a smooth path in life, so prepare to fall, stumble or slip back. However, you must persevere even if it means you must reduce your pace. The most important thing is not to lose sight of the end goal. Learn by Abraham Lincoln who never lost sight of his vision for the future and continued to pursue his goals despite numerous political losses and setbacks.

Don't Quit!

When you are trying to reach the person you want to be the world needs, you are thrown more than a puddle , and hits you with a gigantic or impossible obstacle. This was the case for Handel who was suddenly out of favour, fell into debt and was completely poor before he could write The Messiah. Similar is the case with Thomas Edison whose invention after it was noticed, but not the major breakthrough that he wanted until he created the lamp incandescent.

The path to hell is paved with lofty dreams that never get fulfilled because the people who created these goals gave up and surrendered to fate and fate and. Gandhi could be an accomplished attorney throughout England as well as South Africa if he gave his dreams, but he would not have created the republic that is now independent of India. Mandela might have sat in prison or retreated to an easy life after the incident but the non-apartheid South Africa would not have become a reality.

Never lose hope in the goal you have set. Relax if you need to. Try a different route in case you need to, but don't abandon your goal of becoming the person you want to be. Be persistent. Keep believing and continue to persevere. The end result will be discovering your true self and becoming content.

Love Yourself

If you've reached the level you want to be or are striving to achieve your goals the seeds of true self-love would have been planted. You'd have discovered plenty of reasons to not dislike yourself. You would have accepted the identity of an incarnation and a child of God rather than a random being created by a chemical reaction. You may have discovered potential talents and capabilities that you did not know existed. You may have identified and overcome certain weaknesses in your character and character.

Here are some indications that you've truly began to appreciate yourself:

SELF-CONFIDENCE

Self-confidence refers to a sense of self-assurance in one's capabilities to succeed and achieve something. Even if the result is not a success and the impression persists that you'll do better next time it is a sign of self-confidence.

Self-confidence can be found when you do not feel the necessity of comparing yourself to other people. When you do this, it creates feelings of superiority this is vanity and the start of egotism, conceit, or Narcissism. However should the comparison result into an impression of inferiority and a lack of self-confidence or an absence of self-worth.

Self-confidence builds when you see your own uniqueness as an individual and do not need to compare yourself with other people.

SELF-RESPECT

Self-respect means knowing that you are a distinct person with a unique character characteristics, talents and skills and not just a part within the hive of humankind. It's being able to treat yourself with respect and respect your body.

People who are devoid of self-esteem, don't care about their actions causing offence or if their clothes are in damaged or if substances and substances are harming their bodies. However someone who is self-respectful will take care to look after for their health and diet as well as exercise. They will dress in a manner that allows them to earn the same amount of respect from others , rather than dressing down and appear like a pig. He or she will break off of addiction and endeavor to appear as professional as is possible.

In the most dire of situations, a person with self-esteem will do their best to remain independent and polite, self-reliant, or respectable. It's not clothing, possessions, car, home or job that can earn you self-respect. It's the manner of speaking and attitude that shines through the dirt and strain of everyday life.

SELF-ESTEEM

Self-esteem is the way you demonstrate that you are proud of your self. It can be expressed by an expression of self-confidence, or by a displeasure or even displeasure at your behavior, situation or current situation. Your attitude towards adversity usually the test for the self-esteem you have. If you're angry or unhappy, that usually indicates an absence of self-esteem, unlike when you're optimistic and persevering.

If you are not your true self, you typically seek to get others to feel loved by lowering your own ethics and values. The boundaries you create for yourself are usually an indicator of how much you consider yourself or value yourself as a person. If you take every step needed to safeguard your personal life, stay well and stay out of poor company, it shows the self-esteem you possess and, with it, how much you've learned to cherish yourself.

SELF-FORGIVENESS

The best way to tell if you've learned to be a lover of yourself is when you've admitted your mistakes, apologized and forgiven yourself. Recognizing past mistakes is one aspect. Accepting the responsibility for causing these mistakes is a different. If regrets and the recollections of past mistakes remain in your thoughts despite the repentance and forgiveness given by the authorities, it is time take a step back and allow yourself an opportunity to let go of the past. In the event that it does, it is likely to be a hindrance to becoming a better person and learning to be happy and love.

In addition to the qualities mentioned as such by St Paul, should give you an idea of how well you've come to be a lover of yourself.

All you have to do is to be content.

Be content

Being content is the natural result of learning to appreciate yourself. Being aware of your an immense value and strive to be the person you are supposed to be doesn't mean you need to be miserable and indifferent. If, in fact, you've done everything to become more self-love and you are still not feeling happy could be a sign that you're either avoiding refusing to accept or are unable to accept.

Here are two indicators of happiness that result from truly loving yourself:

Self-assurance

If self-confidence means trusting your capabilities, talents as well as your strength and capability self-assurance means that you know that what you're doing is the right choice and that where you're going is the right direction to be. It is not worrying about making the wrong decision or getting overwhelmed by the challenges and challenges you face.

Self-assurance provides you with the motivation to continue and also the perseverance and endurance to not quit.

Peace of Mind

Happiness is more of a feeling of tranquility than a swell of exuberant laughter. If your mind isn't more weighed down by the past sins or failures and mistakes You are inwardly satisfied. If you can look even your former colleagues or even current adversaries directly at them without a shudder of guilt or fear, this is the hallmark of happiness.

Peace of mind is a result of knowing that you've acknowledged your mistakes and shortcomings and have accepted your mea guilty. It is when you have finished making amends

The Most Loved of All

In this moment, you're likely to feel good about your self. You are confident and feel at confidence in your abilities. You're filled with self-confidence respect, self-confidence and self-confidence. It is possible to say that you've discovered that you love yourself and have become truly content.

But are you?

There is a fine line between the feelings you get from of a narcissistor egotist and a fool with a big ego.

The line of love is by itself.

Returning to St Paul's sermon on love for the Corinthians the Corinthians, he referred to love as nothing more than air flowing through brass instruments, without the qualities of love being used to others, such as being compassionate, suffering long and persevering, believing and bearing without fear of evil, and believing in the truth.

Christ made it clear that He was referring to this in His sermon when He spoke of the second most important commandment , to love your neighbor in the same way as you love yourself, and to be a good neighbor. And as if that weren't not enough, Christ talked about the importance of laying down the life of one's friend in a way that was equal to any other and then went on to make His own model.

Finding the most profound love through discovering your own love doesn't grow more meaningful and significant until you extend that love to other people. Someone anonymous once stated, "Your love for yourself will not be fulfilled until you show it in a the mirror of other people."

Do this and you'll find yourself loving yourself and be happy.

Conclusion

I am very happy to relay this knowledge to you. I am so glad to have learned and may be able to apply these methods in the future.

I hope that this book was capable of helping you comprehend the meaning of self-love and how you can increase your self-love.

Next step would be to start by using this information to hopefully live a happier and joyful life!

Don't be one of those who simply reads the information and does not apply it. the methods that are in this book can only be beneficial if you apply these strategies!

If you know someone who might benefit from the knowledge presented in this book, please let them know about this book.

Thank you for your kind words and best wishes!

www.ingramcontent.com/pod-product-compliance
Lightning Source LLC
Chambersburg PA
CBHW050023130526
44590CB00042B/1839